MW01094122

THE ORVIS POCKET GUIDE TO

Fly Fishing for Stillwater Trout

THE ORVIS POCKET GUIDE TO
Fly Fishing for Stillwater Trout

JIM LEPAGE

Illustrations by Dann Jacobus

The Lyons Press
Guilford, Connecticut
An imprint of The Globe Pequot Press

The Lyons Press is an imprint of The Globe Pequot Press

Printed in China

10 9 8 7 6 5 4 3 2 1

Library of Congress Cataloging-in-Publication Data

Lepage, Jim.
    The Orvis pocket guide to fly fishing for stillwater trout / Jim Lepage; illustrations by Dann Jacobus.
        p. cm.
    ISBN 1-58574-078-0
    1. Trout fishing. 2. Fly fishing. I. Orvis Company. II. Title.

SH687 .L46 2002
799.1′757—dc21

2001050488

CONTENTS

ACKNOWLEDGMENTS

First and foremost to Tom Rosenbauer, who initially gave me this project to work on, coached and cheered me through the initial edits, gave me insight on how I could get it done, and then had the patience to wait me out. Also to Jay Cassell and Bill Bowers at The Lyons Press. In addition, I could never have started to write this book had it not been for many people both in and out of the industry who, over the years, taught me most of what is contained in these pages. Too many to mention but all important, you know who you are. Special mention to Dick Pobst for all his help on entomology; to Charlie Jordan for his coaching and pictures; to Paul Bruun for sharing so many of his still-water experiences; to Don Champion, whose camp in northern Maine has been a major stillwater base for twenty years; to Wayne MacDougall and Dan Harrison, good friends and fanatical fishermen, and many others, all of whom continue to inspire and make my fishing experiences special. Especially to Dad and my son Brian, as many of my fondest memories and experiences have been shared with one, the other, or both for many years. I look forward to seeing all of you on a special stillwater soon.

DEDICATION

To Debbie, Megan, Nicole, and Brian for their support all these years.

To Dad, who helped inspire my fishing experiences growing up, and to my son Brian. You both are my best friends and fishing companions.

To Tom Rosenbauer, friend and fishing partner, who continually told me I could do this, and then taught me how.

To my friends and fishing companions who, over the years, learned and experienced with me the wonderful world of fly fishing, and continue to do so.

INTRODUCTION

Readily accessible to all anglers, stillwater fly fishing can be a destination traveled to or a walk in your backyard. While rivers and streams can be crowded with anglers, stillwater by definition is silent, tranquil, hushed, subdued, free from disturbance or agitation, and free of noticeable current. Memories of sunrises and sunsets, mirrored images on a dead-still pond or lake, and the dimpled rings of rising fish are all a part of stillwater fly fishing. Although you'll share many great experiences with other anglers on stillwaters, you will also be able to hike into a seemingly unfished pond teeming with brightly colored trout that have never seen another angler.

Stillwater fly fishing can be a beginner's playground or an advanced angler's challenge. Like a body of salt water, a large lake can be intimidating without the right knowledge, but a little knowledge goes a long way in making this experience a rewarding one. It's like the 80/20 rule: The most important 20 percent of what there is to learn will result in taking 80 percent of the fish. That leaves a lot to learn for the remaining 20 percent of the fish, some of which may be the largest in the pond, but makes for a great jump start in getting to know any stillwater you have your sights on. The basic knowledge required to fish stillwater is the same

Even large waters like this can be broken down into smaller sections likely to produce trout.

for any lake or pond; the remaining knowledge base comprises the idiosyncrasies of the stillwater you are fishing, and must be learned on your own.

The misconception that stillwater fly fishing requires long casts and technical presentations to take trout is just not true. Anglers who have spent their lives on stillwater will tell you of countless times when trout took a fly only a few feet away, and others when a ninety-foot cast covering a rise resulted in refusal. No matter what your level of mastery, fishing stillwaters will continually offer new experiences and conditions to help hone your skills.

Small stillwaters like this, though not as intimidating, require stealth and cunning to produce trout.

This guide will give you the information you need to approach any stillwater confidently and with the skill to catch fish. No matter where you are fishing, this book will give you the tools and techniques needed to make your stillwater fishing experience a rewarding one. The rest is up to you.

JIM LEPAGE

PART ONE

TACKLE AND GEAR

It's important to start with equipment before leaping into fishing strategies. I have seen too many anglers who did not take the time to outfit themselves correctly. The cost of not spending time reviewing your tackle needs could be a lost fish, the wrong flies, the wrong rod for the line or conditions, or even worse, a bad experience. Set your mind at ease and make sure you're prepared before you go off on your fishing vacation by getting the right gear for the trout you are seeking.

Using the right gear will help you bring to net trophy trout like this nice brown.

FLY RODS

Your choice of rod is certainly one of the most important choices you will need to make but is also one of the simplest. I know you will go through your own internal struggles on cost, but it only hurts once to find a good rod. A bad rod that ruins a trip will cost you dearly. As you choose your rod keep in mind that we are focusing on trout fishing as opposed to panfish and bass. Trout are the most sought-after species in stillwater fly fishing.

The most common rod in stillwater fishing for trout is a nine-foot 6-weight, and if you are buying your first rod this should be your rod of choice. I know many

Whether you're casting from shore, boat, canoe, or float tube, a nine-foot rod for a 6-weight line will cover all your stillwater needs.

skilled anglers who profess that a nine-foot 5-weight is a great stillwater rod, but these same anglers quickly grab a 6-weight when conditions change. My personal choice for trout fishing on stillwaters is the nine-foot 6-weight; I don't leave home without it. It has the ability to cast large wind-resistant dry flies and streamer patterns into the wind, yet can also present small drys to finicky trout. These simple examples of the versatility of a nine-foot 6-weight rod are reason enough to purchase one.

There are situations that make other rods, maybe ones you already own, suitable for stillwater fishing. When fishing from a stable boat an eight-and-a-half-foot rod for a 6-weight can be a good choice. Because you are higher above the water when casting (many times able to stand while casting) you do not need a longer rod. However, a short rod is a disadvantage in float tubes or canoes, as being closer to the water's surface can cause rise rings to form behind you, not from fish but rather from your line hitting the water, a frustrating experience.

When fishing from a float tube a nine-and-a-half or ten-foot rod for a 6-weight is a good choice. Because you're close to the water during casting, the extra rod length helps keep your line off the water, especially during backcasts. It becomes a disadvantage in high wind as the extra rod length is exposed to higher resistance and makes you push harder when casting.

When fishing from a canoe a nine-foot rod for 6-weight is a good choice. You are sitting higher out of the water than when in a float tube, but still do not have the ability to stand while casting. This makes a nine-foot rod the perfect rod for fishing from a canoe.

Refer to the chart below for choosing a rod for various fishing situations and species. Although this book targets the trout fishery, I have included some other recommendations should you be looking for a rod that covers other fishing situations.

ROD/ LINE WT	8½′	9′	9½′	10′
4 wt	Panfish from boats	Panfish from canoe, shore, or boat	Panfish from a float tube, shore, or canoe	Panfish from a float tube
5 wt	Small trout from boats	Small trout from canoe, shore, or boat	Small trout from float tube, shore, or canoe	Small trout from float tube
6 wt	Large trout from boats	Large trout from canoe, shore, or boat	Large trout from float tube, shore, or canoe	Large trout from float tube
7 wt	Smallmouth bass from boat	Smallmouth bass from canoe, shore, or boat	Smallmouth bass from float tube, shore, or canoe	Smallmouth bass from float tube
8 wt	Largemouth bass from boats	Largemouth bass from canoe, shore, or boat	Largemouth bass from float tube, shore, or canoe	Largemouth bass from float tube

REELS

Depending on the stillwater you are fishing and the size of the fish you expect to catch, the reel you put on your rod can do a variety of jobs for you while you are bringing in the catch of the day. Basically, though, it stores fly line and backing. When you are preparing to cast, you pull the amount of fly line off the reel that you intend to fish with, and the reel stores the rest until you want to either pull more line off or put line back on. There are many different types of reels, with different coatings, size ranges, price ranges, shapes, drags, handles, and knobs. But remember the reel is basically doing what I described above, holding your line until either you or the fish decides to take it off, but only you can decide when to put it back on.

When a big fish heads for the bottom or the middle of the pond, it's crucial to have a reel you can count on.

During a recent outing in Montana's Glacier National Park on Duck Lake, which is known for its huge rainbow trout, I was helping a beginner learn to spot fish cruising the bank. While trying to hook one of these monsters, she did everything right. The fish took, and headed for the middle of the lake. The reel was a spring-and-pawl, she had no experience palming reels, and trying to teach someone palming techniques when a seven-pound Montana rainbow is heading for Idaho is not easy. She landed the fish but not until the trout was a couple of turns from taking all her backing. A disk-drag reel would have taken care of this fish in short order. Stepping up to basic disk-drag models will help when chasing large trout.

FLY LINES

The right fly line is the most critical choice of tackle in stillwater fly fishing. Since it covers many different fishing depths, from the water's surface to depths of twenty feet (see sketch), the fly line is your only means of getting a fly to where the trout are. You will need at least two lines to accomplish this in most stillwater fishing applications, a floating line and a sinking line.

Floating

For many stillwater fishermen, casting to rising trout conjures up thoughts of quiet evenings on mirror-calm stillwaters dimpled with rings as trout slurp emerging mayflies. There is nothing quite as rewarding as cast-

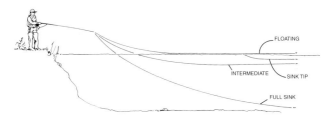

Many different fly lines are available, including floating, intermediate, sink-tip, and full-sinking lines. Using the right line allows you to fish at any depth necessary.

ing to a rising trout, watching him slowly rise to meet your fly with open mouth, and lifting your rod to meet with the resistance of his bulky form. In these situations a good floating line is a must-have item and one that will make your stillwater experience rewarding. Floating fly lines come in various tapers and colors. A standard weight-forward taper in a high-visibility color, like yellow, is the most common and the one I would recommend. Floating lines are most often used for dry flies, emergers, and occasionally streamers in early spring or late fall when fish are feeding close to shore or near the water's surface.

Sinking

To other stillwater anglers, retrieving a fly on choppy days to trout that dwell and feed in deep water is what it's all about. In fact, you cannot fish effectively in 90 percent of stillwater situations without a sinking line. Most trout feeding takes place subsurface (possibly as much as 90 percent) making a sinking line and/or flies fished below the water's surface productive in most fishing situations. The feeling of the unanticipated yank as a trout inhales the fly that swings off the bottom to imitate the emergence of a mayfly about to surface, the head shake of an unseen fish after you set the hook, is what stillwater angling is all about. In these situations a sinking fly line is a must-have item. These lines, like floating lines, come in various tapers, but the colors available are limited due to the materials used to make them sink. Because tungsten is most commonly used in making full-sinking lines nowadays, and tungsten in raw form is a dark gray powder, the line color range is from dark green to black. The faster the sink rate of the line you are using, the darker the line color. Because stillwaters are flat calm during evening hatches on only a few precious, lucky, and rare days in a season, a sinking line becomes a stillwater fly fisher's best friend.

Basic nymphs, emergers, and streamers that imitate baitfish or crayfish, and attractor patterns are best fished with sinking lines. I probably fish full-sinking lines four to one over floating lines. I recommend a full-sinking line in a class III (sink rate of two to three inches per second) or a class V (sink rate of five to six inches per second). If I had only one line to take it would be the class V. It gets to the bottom quicker than other full-sinking lines. Make sure when buying a full-sinking line that it is density compensated. This means that the line is designed to sink at the same rate throughout its taper so that it does not form a belly as it sinks.

Specialty

Specialty lines including sink tips, Sly Lines (clear monocore "slime" lines), and intermediate sinking lines all can come in handy in certain situations. Of all the specialty lines available today, the one that I use the most is the Orvis Depth Charge fly line. It has a thirty foot extra-fast-sinking head attached to a running line made with an intermediate coating. It sinks like a stone, getting deep in a hurry. The intermediate line follows the sinking head down more easily than a floating running line. I will often substitute the Depth Charge line in place of my full-sinking line, as it is a more versatile tool for fishing deep water. Depth Charge is not sold by line weight, but rather grain weight. I recommend the 200-grain Depth Charge for 5-weight rods and the 250-grain for 6-weight.

The only other line that I recommend for use in fishing subsurface nymphs or streamers close to the water's surface is the Sly Line. This line is manufactured using a single-strand monocore with a clear PVC coating, and is completely transparent. It sinks slowly, leaving no wake as you retrieve it. It is a great line when casting to spooky fish along a shore where you're concerned with lining a fish. "Lining a fish" means spooking it as a result of casting your line over the fish or in its vicinity. If they see the shadow or splash of the line as it hits the water, fish will quickly take cover. A Sly Line is narrow in diameter so it lands on the water with little disturbance, casts very little shadow, and is clear rather than opaque when re-

trieved. I like to use a Sly Line if I am casting streamers close to the shore or along the water's surface, as it
increases my chances of catching fish that are between
me and my fly during the retrieve.

LEADERS

Leaders come in a variety of lengths, tapers, and diameters, in either knotless or knotted form. If I were to
pick one leader that works in most all situations, a
nine-foot knotless tapered leader in a 4X or 5X diameter would be my choice. Most companies' manufactured leader tapers will do the job, but some do not

On calm days, long leaders with fine tippets are the key to taking finicky
trout.

On windy days, when a chop breaks up the water's surface, a slightly shorter leader and heavier tippet are sufficient, as the trout are less spooky.

have good tapers. Make sure the leader you are using has a taper and comes from a reputable company that has done its homework on designs. If you are buying a leader for the first time, look for a heavier butt section, followed by a section that tapers to a fine-diameter level tippet. Knotless leaders are manufactured by being extruded through special machines to give them exacting tapers for turnover and presentation. They are then set with heat and tension so that their breaking strength increases as you go from the thin tippet that attaches to your fly to the thick butt that connects your fly line to the leader. Knotted leaders are made of various level sections of line, starting with heavy material at the butt and tapering to the thin tippet. A knotted leader could have as many as eight or nine knots from start to finish. Knotted leaders have several major faults. First, the knots are prone to breakage. Also, they snag small pieces of grass or debris, often leaving an unwanted wake when retrieved. Spending time cleaning this off is time you could be fishing, and with debris attached during the retrieve your chances of catching a fish are reduced. There is no reason to use anything other than knotless leaders for your fly fishing.

In addition to the above information there are materials available that you need to be aware of. Nylon is the most commonly used material for leaders. Formulation changes in nylon will change a leader's breaking strength, abrasion resistance, elongation, color, or tenacity. Many companies sell several formulas to cover a range of fishing applications, but will point you in the direction of the best to use for trout fishing. In recent years a material called PVDF or polyvinylidene fluoride, often called fluorocarbon, has hit the market. It is expensive but its attributes deserve to be noted. Its breaking strength is usually less than that of a comparable nylon material, but it does not absorb water, which reduces a material's breaking strength. Nylon can absorb as much as 20 to 25 percent water, which reduces its breaking strength significantly. PVDF also has a refractive index that is very close to water's, which means it reflects light at about the same angle as water does. This allows the material to virtually disappear when being fished, one of its greatest advantages. Its abrasion resistance is also better than that of most nylons. Although this material is denser than nylon and therefore sinks quicker, I have used it for dry-fly fishing for over five years and wouldn't change. With the help of the fly's ability to float and water tension it can readily be used for dry-fly fishing. I normally use a nylon leader with piece of PVDF tippet material blood-knotted to the end of my leader. I also find that when using PVDF it is possible to go up one X size in tippet diameter. Because of its invisibility in water it is less apt to be seen by finicky trout. I can honestly say that this material has increased my ability to catch fish. On some especially tough days, fishing next to better fishermen, I have been able to outfish them three to one. Without PVDF this would not have been possible.

Your leader length should be varied based on the type of fishing you are doing. Here is some advice on leaders and which ones to use in various situations:

Leaders less than nine feet in length (six to seven-and-a-half feet) are great for sinking fly lines where you want the fly to stay with your line as it sinks. Nylon material has a specific gravity that makes it just a little heavier than water, whereas a sinking line can be many times denser than water. Longer leaders tend to prevent the fly from sinking at the same rate as the fly line. This causes a belly to form in the line (see sketch) and can cause missed strikes, as it is hard to set the hook when your line forms a semicircle in the water. Shorter leaders will allow your fly to stay closer to the tip of your fly line as it sinks, keeping your line, leader, and fly at

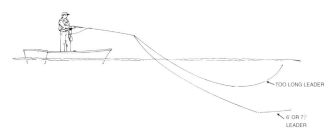

TOO LONG LEADER

6' OR 7½' LEADER

Using too long a leader with a sinking line can form a belly in the line and prevent you from feeling strikes. Use a shorter leader to keep fly and line at the same level.

about the same depth during the retrieve. This enhances your ability to set the hook, as the fly line and fly are more directly in line with the fish as it strikes.

I would recommend six-foot leaders for most sinking line applications unless water clarity is really good, and then I would go to a seven-and-a-half-foot leader for these conditions. Leaders that are nine feet in length are about average and are most often used for standard dry-fly fishing and retrieving subsurface nymphs or streamers when using a floating line. Both water clarity and your fly size should be your guide to which leader you will use on stillwater. If I am casting No. 12 or larger dry-fly I use a nine-foot leader. Longer leaders of 12, 15, or 18 feet in small diameters (from 4X to 7X) can twist the tippet, as the air-resistant fly wants to spin during casting. When casting large dry flies like *Hexagenia* mayflies that are often a No. 6 or 8, you need to go to either a nine-foot 3X leader or seven-and-a-half-foot 4X to prevent this twisting.

Leaders that are 12, 15, and 18 feet offer some stealth when fishing to finicky trout and are usually available only in smaller diameters from 4X to 7X. Often on calm days or clear waters, the fly line can easily spook fish when it comes too close to them as your fly is being presented. A longer tapered leader presents your fly at a greater distance from the fly line, allowing for less disturbance of the water and a better presentation to those spooky fish. Longer leaders can become challenging when casting into even a slight wind, so depending on the application, you may have to go from a fifteen-foot to a twelve-foot leader in order to get the turnover you are looking for. I most often fish a twelve-foot leader as a standard length when fishing to rising trout.

Leader diameters are normally referred to in X size ranges. For the most part, the diameters can be determined by the flies you cast. In the chart I have listed the X size range, the diameters associated with these sizes, and the sizes of flies that are recommended for use with each. The diameter of the leader (rated in X sizes) you are using is more important than the pound test rating when choosing leaders for trout fishing.

TIPPET MATERIAL

Tippet material is used either to replace or add to the tippet section of the leader. In the process of replacing flies over a period of time your leader will be shortened and the diameter will start to increase once you have used up the tippet section and start cutting into the taper. Simply tie on a piece of tippet material using a surgeon's or blood knot, and you're back in business. It sure beats replacing your leader each time you get to this point. I often buy a nylon leader in a nine-foot length and 4X (.007 inch diameter) and add three feet of 5X (.006 inch diameter) PVDF material to this leader, making it twelve feet in length with a PVDF tippet section. A full PVDF leader is expensive, yet a spool of PVDF tippet material can turn any nylon leader into a PVDF leader by just adding a few feet to your leader. After all, the section tied to your fly is the critical part of the leader. With a

Tippet Size	Diameter	Balances with Fly Sizes
0X	.011	2, 1/0
1X	.010	4, 6, 8
2X	.009	6, 8, 10
3X	.008	10, 12, 14
4X	.007	12, 14, 16
5X	.006	14, 16, 18
6X	.005	16, 18, 20, 22
7X	.004	18, 20, 22, 24
8X	.003	22, 24, 26, 28

Chart showing recommended leader diameters for different fly sizes.

twenty-five-yard spool of PVDF I can change approximately twenty-five leaders into "stealth" leaders for fishing stillwater. That makes the investment worthwhile.

WADERS

Today breathable waders far outsell the neoprene waders of yesterday. Their ease of movement, comfort, and breathability make them the best choice. I may use neoprene for a winter steelheading trip, but 99 percent of the time I am in breathable waders.

Breathable waders can make hiking in to reach a pond or lake a sweat-free pleasure. If you plan to do any walking along shorelines that have thick brush or trees, get a pair with double fabric overlays on the knee and shin areas. A pair that has a durable, puncture-resistant outer layer of fabric will help prevent briars or sharp branches from punching a hole in your waders. I also like to be able to roll my chest-high waders down to waist high. Some companies offer chest models that can be transformed into waist-high waders by simply rolling them down, with the shoulder straps transforming into a belt. These are great for hot days and shallow wading along shorelines. Most companies offer a wide range of waders with these options for fly fishermen. Whether boot-foot or stocking-foot, make sure the waders meet your needs. For wading safety, a belt should always be purchased if it is not included with the waders.

Today's breathable waders are a great way to stay comfortable, dry, and with proper layering, warm even in very cold water.

SUNGLASSES

Simply speaking, if you leave these at home, go back and get them. Polarized (key word) sunglasses do more than just help you to see into the water. They drastically reduce eyestrain by preventing you from squinting either from direct sunlight or from reflections off the water's surface. They also keep wind and debris from entering your eyes on those windy days. In addition, as an added bonus, they may actually allow you to spot fish. Lens color makes a big difference in

Stalking and catching this gorgeous rainbow would not have been possible without the aid of good polarized sunglasses.

your ability to spot fish; I recommend copper or amber as the best color for spotting fish in lakes and ponds.

How are you going to fish that pond you have always looked at, or the one your buddy wants to take you to? The preparation, techniques, and equipment will vary with each approach. Here are a few tips about the methods most commonly used for fishing stillwaters.

FISHING FROM A BOAT

If you are fishing from a boat, anything from a rowboat to a Boston Whaler, you have the ability to stand while casting. I like a slightly shorter eight-and-a-half-foot rod when I am standing in a boat. Shorter rods are less affected by wind and have leverage advantages when bringing fish to the boat. A boat offers several advantages over other methods of fishing stillwater, including storage of gear, and stability during casting. Also, boats are safe and sturdy. Disadvantages can be lack of stealth (boats can be noisy in water during navigation and stalking), and although boats provide a very mobile means of fishing, getting the boat onto many remote (and some not-so-remote) stillwaters can be problematic. Make sure to check the area you are about to fish to make sure there is a launch capable of handling the boat you are going to bring.

I once took a trip to a remote pond in Maine, where in order to fish the pond you had to travel twenty-six miles on remote logging roads, with the last mile of road all but impassable to anything except a four-wheel-drive vehicle. The pond access was a footpath

An angler casts to a rise from a stable boat that allows him to stand and move about safely.

about thirty yards from the water. The largest motor I had ever seen on this beautiful lake was a five-horsepower and even that was rare. I arrived at the pond and was shocked to find a truck trailering a bass boat with a two-hundred-horsepower Chrysler V6 outboard on the back. They had taken a chain saw and decided to cut a trail to the lake so that they could try to get their boat in. They had cut the trail about halfway when a game warden showed up and, to the surprise of the fishermen, wrote them a ticket with a very stiff fine for cutting trees to the lake. They were lucky they got out of there with their boat and truck still in their possession. The warden was much nicer than I would have been. A little planning on their part would have alerted them to this problem, but there is no excuse for damaging an area by cutting your way to the lake or pond. Please remember to leave an area in better condition than when you arrived. This will allow you and others to enjoy the spot for many years to come. There are public boat launches on plenty of area lakes and ponds; use them.

Additionally, when fishing from boats, make sure the proper life preservers are available on board. You never know when you will need them and by law they must be stowed for easy access. I recommend two anchors when fishing from a boat or canoe. They should be tied fore and aft (bow and stern, or front and back for you landlubbers) so that you can position the boat and tie them off once you have the anchors in the correct spot. They will keep your boat from spinning or moving with the wind (See sketch). A wind moving

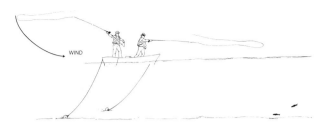

WIND

Proper placement of two anchors is critical to fish effectively from a boat on windy days.

from right to left, if you are a right-handed caster, is not a good wind unless you have become proficient at ducking as the fly whistles by your head. Try to position your boat so that the wind is your friend, not your enemy. If you are using oars instead of a motor, a spare oar in the boat helps if one breaks or is lost during your fishing. If you use a motor make sure that oars are on the boat, they fit the oarlocks, and they are in good working order before you go onto the lake. I have helped many boaters who had a motor fail while on a lake or pond, and had no oars to help them get back to where they started.

CANOES

Canoes are a common means of fishing stillwater and one of my favorites. Canoes are portable, easily carried on a vehicle, and allow you to cover large areas of water quietly. When I talk about canoes I am speaking of craft of eighteen feet or less, not rated for motors.

This angler may be putting himself in danger by standing in his canoe.

There are larger Grand Lake–style canoes that I consider boats, as they will take a ten-horsepower motor, and must be trailered to the water. For lakes and ponds, a canoe of sixteen to eighteen feet is ideal. A flat bottom helps with stability, and a keel keeps the canoe on course when the wind picks up.

Standing is not recommended in a canoe and can put you and your partner, if you are fishing with one, in an unsafe situation. Thus I prefer a nine-foot 6-weight rod. Casting from a sitting position takes some getting used to. I have found that a stripping basket kept on the floor of the canoe is great for keeping your line tangle free when casting. Put the basket between your legs in a position where it is comfortable for you to strip line into when retrieving. When you cast your line again you will find the stripping basket prevents it from getting caught under your shoes, around the end of the oar, on your backpack, or on any other snag it can find. A basket really helps to make casting from a canoe a good experience, and most important it allows you to spend more time fishing as opposed to untangling line.

When anchoring a canoe, like boat fishing, you should have two anchors to put yourself in the proper position for casting. If fishing by yourself, adjust the weight in the canoe so that it is evenly distributed to help you navigate. There are a couple of ways to accomplish this. I like to sit in the front of the canoe facing the back. This puts my body more toward the center of the canoe and therefore makes the canoe stay flat and easier to maneuver. If your canoe does not allow you to do this, a rock or backpack placed in the front of the canoe will accomplish the same thing.

With a little practice, canoe fishing can be very effective. This nice trout came from a stillwater in Maine.

If fishing two people, keep in mind that the person sitting in the rear of the canoe is often casting across the canoe to the water situated on the left side (if you're right-handed). This means that your line is passing dangerously close to the person in the front of the canoe. It is possible to swivel around slightly and cast to the right side. This is a much safer casting position for the person in the rear, as it minimizes the possibility of hooking your partner.

Many areas have laws that require the use of a life vest. There are some very slim-profile vests out there that will make your canoe experience a comfortable one while assuring your safety should something happen and you find yourself treading water. I have been fishing out of canoes for thirty years, and have even done some whitewater and stillwater racing over the years. Yet, I found myself upside down with a good friend just this past season. It doesn't make any difference how, it's just important to know that it can happen when you least expect it.

FLOAT TUBES

Float tubes are quiet and stealthy, and easily packed into a pond or lake either fully inflated or folded in a pack basket. They can be inflated with a foot pump once you have arrived at the stillwater you are fishing. They are also slow moving, a bit awkward, and low to the water when casting. Tubes are great for hikes into remote ponds where you can't cast from shore and the fish always seem to be out of reach. I have seen fishermen in tubes wearing headset walkie-talkies like fighter pilots, discussing the next sortie and what to use on the next attack. It's a fun way to stay in touch with your partner while keeping up on areas that are producing or flies that seem to be working.

A good set of fins is a must, as they are your only means of propulsion besides the wind, which usually blows in the direction you don't want to go! Beware of leg cramps when you are tubing. During the first few trips of the season or when tubing for an entire day,

Float tubes can allow an angler to hike in to remote ponds, or to fish parts of a pond not easily reached from shore.

finning can strain your legs, especially when this is a new means of fishing. It is a painful experience so take it easy and don't overextend yourself on the first couple of trips. I find the U-boat-style tubes to be the most comfortable. They allow you to keep your legs out in front of you; this position is the most comfortable position for fishing and finning.

Chest-high breathable waders that allow freedom of movement will make kicking the fins a little easier. Also, high-back waders help to keep water from entering.

Since you are sitting so close to the water (actually in it), keeping your cast off the surface becomes a challenge, thus the need for longer rods. I recommend a 5-wt or 6-weight, nine-and-a-half or ten-foot rod for tubing. You will find these longer rods are great for sensitivity, tippet protection, and for keeping your back-cast off the water. They are a bit of a challenge in a high wind and when trying to get fish close enough to net, but the attributes far outweigh the challenges.

Float tubing can be a challenge and you must be careful of where you are venturing off to. If you are covering a large body of water your access area can be very important. Getting from point A to point B can take a while if your destination lies on the other side of the lake or pond from where you start. Float tubes are great for those small ponds that can easily be covered in a day, or for areas within a half mile of your access area. The wind is the biggest problem encountered when tubing, so be aware of the direction you and the wind are going. It can quickly turn against you if you have ventured too far out onto a big body of water and now want to get back to where you started. If you start your day working into the wind it will be easier at the end of the day, when you're tired, to go with the wind to get back to your starting point. I have also on occasion dropped off my gear, shuttled my truck to the downwind side, hiked back to my tube, and then proceeded to fish my way to the other side and my truck without having to worry about working into the wind. No matter how you decide to do it, I recommend keeping the wind in mind.

Here's a helpful hint that I find makes my float tubing easier and safer. Take a flat, square, Coast Guard–approved boat cushion and put it on the seat of the float tube. Then when putting the float tube apron

Remember to check wind direction and carefully note your starting point as you set out in a float tube.

around you, pass the clips through the handles of the boat cushion. This keeps the cushion in place while you fish. The cushion does two things for you: It allows you to sit further up out of the water for casting and fishing (for short guys like me, this is a great advantage), and it acts as a safety device should you run into any deflation problems while in the tube. In some states it is the law that life preservers be worn while in a float tube. Consult the local regulations in the area you plan to fish to make sure you conform to these requirements.

For float tubes a single anchor works well to maintain position. Where you tie off the anchor on your tube and the direction of the wind will determine what position you end up in for fishing. Small, compact anchors that fit into a side pocket work well and can be clipped onto a number of D rings around the tube to easily put you in position to cover water. I also find that a catch-and-release net is worth having readily available for landing fish in a tube. The fish are easier to handle, and a net helps you catch, handle, and release fish in less time.

WADING

Some ponds can be fished easily from shore, either by wading or just by walking the shoreline. If there is room for casting and access is good, this can be a great way to fish any stillwater, as trout cruise along the shorelines looking for food and can be sought easily

Wading shorelines is an easy, productive way to fish stillwaters, especially during spring and fall on large stillwaters like this one in Maine.

from shore instead of having to bring a float tube or boat. If this is the case, a pair of waders can allow you either to fish from shore or wade into areas where you can cast to fish feeding a little further out in deeper water. Breathable waders are the ticket! They allow for comfortable, sweat-free hiking into ponds and keep you dry while wading.

PART TWO

FISHING THE SEASONS

It is a mistake to think that stillwater fisheries are all the same. Their locations, depths, coves, structures, inlets and outlets, size, water clarity, insect life, shorelines, seasons, and more create diverse and unique habitats that differentiate each and every stillwater. They have at least as much, if not more, diversity as rivers and streams. Fundamentally, stillwater differs from rivers or streams in its noticeable current characteristics. Keep in mind I said "noticeable." The wind, inlets, outlets, and springs will indeed cause currents that are not often apparent when looking at a stillwater fishery. Not until you fish these areas will you start to notice these currents, and they will change with the season, the month, or even from day to day as water temperatures or weather change. Likewise, the fish do not react the same. Where often in rivers and streams fish can be found in the same run, pool, or riffle year after year, stillwater trout can be found anywhere looking for food or a water temperature that suits the season. Because of this, it is important to understand what to look for during different times of the year, and during different times of the day. Once you know what to look for seasonally, you can start to analyze structure, drop-offs, inlets, weed beds, hatches, water temperatures, weather, and any other variables that you will need to be aware of in order to make your stillwater experience a valuable one.

SPRING

Spring, in many eastern or northern stillwaters, marks the beginning of the fishing season, while in western and southern areas it represents a continuation of a year-round fishery. In most all areas around the United States spring brings a change in fishing as runoff, warmer water, and migration of both gamefish and baitfish cause increased feeding activity. Trout and landlocked salmon in the Northeast can be extremely aggressive in springtime. In the Northeast, Upper Midwest, or any areas where winter brings ice formation and spring brings a thaw, the spring season can be a wild one. The immediate loss of ice from a stillwater is often followed by a flurry of activity that some (myself included) believe is prompted by increased oxygenation of the surface waters through exposure to air. Along with a dramatic shift in the water's layers, in which cooler water from the surface of the pond sinks deeper, fish move into shallow areas along shorelines or shoals, and feeding activity increases. Because of baitfish spawning activity, the inlets and outlets of many stillwaters become prime locations for taking feeding trout that are aggressively crashing bait and gulping their stunned quarry. Activity during the spring, no matter where you are, will be centered along the shorelines, around inlets and outlets, near rocky

On northern stillwaters, ice-out marks the beginning of another season. It can also mean some great early trout fishing.

shallow shoals, and on the surface. Spring also marks the beginning of increased insect activity within many stillwaters across the United States. As the longer days of spring start to warm the shallow areas and shorelines, caddis, mayflies, and midges get active, so trout cruise and feed on and near the surface. At this time of year, rising fish can be found any time of day, as comfortable water temperatures bring trout to shallow areas and to the surface.

SUMMER

As spring fades to summer, water temperatures at the surface and along the shorelines start to rise. Cooler early morning and evening temperatures may bring fish into the shallows or up to the surface looking for

In summer, fishing early in the morning can be the key to finding actively feeding trout.

food. So, although finding rising fish during this time of year is not an all-day affair, it can be productive if you're going early or staying late. Fish have moved to deeper water and are holding in layers that may be twenty feet down or more. Sinking lines and nymphs or streamers are a must in order to be successful during daytime hours. This is when spring-fed ponds can produce great fishing if you've done your homework. Remember: Fish have not stopped feeding when activity seems to be at a lull during the summer doldrums. They have simply moved to cooler water and are not as dispersed as during spring, winter, and fall. Knowing where to look for fish during these apparently slow times can bring about great fishing when most people are home waiting for the seasons to change.

When cloudy, rainy weather shows up in midsummer, a Depth Charge full-sinking line can result in great action, as fish become more active in foul weather.

FALL

As summer moves toward fall it is amazing how few nights of low temperatures are needed to see fishing activity increase. As water temperatures at the surface start to decrease, fish disperse and activity in stillwater starts to take on new meaning. Fish cruise more readily during the morning and evening hours. On cloudy days this activity will often last all day. By midfall, fishing is similar to springtime action. Feeding fish are often caught bashing schooled-up baitfish against the shorelines (this is called a "fry bash" in England) in early evening and can be fooled into taking a streamer stripped through these stunned bait pods. Insect hatches in the fall may not be as prolific as in late spring or early summer, but you *will* find trout back on the surface when emerging insects are active. Concentrate some of your fishing time on inlets and outlets, as

In the fall, pond outlets can quickly turn on, especially if late-season rains bring the water levels up.

these areas also become productive. Browns, brookies, and cutthroat trout are readying themselves for the spawn, while rainbows tag along to feed on the eggs dislodged during spawning.

While fall nymphing can be extraordinary, pre-spawn trout often change their feeding habits, and a brightly colored attractor pattern or large dry fly can be productive during this time of year. Yellow Leeches stripped in quickly will bring some wild strikes, while Stimulators, Elkhair Caddis, and large Wulff dry flies, fished in the tailouts, will often bring fish off the bottom to inhale your offering.

WINTER

Winter in many areas means pulling out the ice-fishing gear, but southern and western stillwaters have great winter fishing. Water temperatures in these warmer areas stay fairly uniform during this time of year, allowing for the use of spring or fall techniques, as fish will be found cruising the shallows and surface areas. In colder climates, but in areas where ice has still not formed, winter takes on a phenomenon similar to summer, but reversed: Water temperatures are too cold in the shallows and at the surface to promote feeding activity. In these situations the most comfortable layer has again moved deeper, but instead of moving from warm summer water temperatures, the trout are moving to escape the cold winter water. Using sinking lines and concentrating your efforts along deep drop-offs and structure will produce the majority of the ac-

Western stillwaters can produce some intense fishing in winter. During this trip to Colorado we managed some of the best trout fishing we have ever seen. (*Tom Rosenbauer photo*)

tion. If you happen to be fishing a warm sunny day, you may find shallow-water areas warming up to temperatures that bring about some insect activity. If this happens, look in the shallow coves and along shorelines, as trout may start cruising these areas looking for active insects.

SPRING-FED PONDS AND SEASONAL VARIATIONS

All stillwaters are affected by seasonal variations, although some are more affected than others. For instance, a spring-fed pond will be affected less than a pond or stillwater with a stream inlet and outlet. Water levels in spring-fed ponds typically change little, even in a very dry season, due to their unvarying spring sources. Depending on the number of springs and the size of the stillwater, I have found that trout habits within these spring areas vary little despite these seasonal changes. Surface and shoreline temperatures will be affected, but layer changes within the spring-fed areas at various depths are minimized due to the constant temperature of the water being supplied. Spring-fed ponds are comparable to tailwater rivers or spring creeks. Of all stream and river fishing available around the world, tailwaters and spring creeks are the most consistent year-round fisheries. They maintain uniform water temperatures, thereby keeping insect activity high and trout feeding steadily throughout the year. This is also true of spring-fed ponds.

Finding the springs within the pond can be a valuable resource for a stillwater fisherman, especially if there are only one or two springs feeding the pond or lake. There are a couple of ways to spot springs in these fisheries. A plane flying low over a pond can clearly spot the springs in shallow mountain ponds. Often marked by a lighter-colored bottom or vegetation, they can be seen and marked on maps. If you live in a cold climate where ponds, lakes, or beaver ponds freeze in the winter, an area of open water or soft ice, which show up as darker spots on frozen stillwaters, will reveal the springs. During open-water months I carry a thermometer attached to a thirty-foot lead with a digital readout. I can drop the weighted thermometer to the bottom of the pond and start paddling slowly around the pond until I see a drop in water temperature, indicating a spring. I mark this spot, and back

Spring-fed stillwaters are often a challenge to fish. Spend some time taking in the beauty of these areas while looking for access points or rising trout.

away so I am positioned to cast into the spring. I once found a good-size spring on a great mountain pond where I would anchor up and fish for trout. An occasional boat would appear to fish the same pond and they would see me bringing in trout fairly regularly. They would ask what I was using and I would tell them the fly, and even give them some so they would be using the same pattern. They would go off happy for the information but still remain troutless. I always keep my spring information quiet, because in many ponds there is only one spring. The fishing is best in springs during the hot summer doldrums. The fish congregate close to these spring areas and often vacate other areas of the pond. A fly fisherman who can find these springs can often catch trout when other anglers are working hard for little or no action.

PART THREE

TECHNIQUES AND STRATEGIES

When approaching a stillwater you will find that there are really only three fishing situations you will find yourself in: You will be prospecting the pond for fish, fishing a fly or technique that mimics something you have observed while on the water, or you'll be in the middle of a hatch. Other variables including weather, time of year, the size of stillwater, fishing methods used, and more will affect your fishing, but you will still find yourself in one of these three situations.

STILLWATER PROSPECTING

More often than not I find myself on a stillwater with no apparent hatches to give away the trouts' location. Fear not, this does not mean the trout are not feeding. In fact, studies estimate that anywhere from 80 to 95 percent of a trout's diet is subsurface. I see this as an opportunity to prospect for trout as opposed to kicking back and waiting for trout to start rising. It's more interesting when fisherman leave or turn around to go home when they see no evidence of rising fish. I can confidently tell you that I have taken many more trout subsurface than on top with drys. I can also tell you that windy, churned-up water has the potential to produce more fish than a pond that is lying still, although

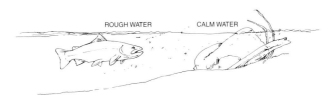

On windy days, rough water can stir up food, and trout will often feed in the lee of a point or rock. Feeding can happen both at and below the surface.

either situation offers a good prospecting opportunity when fishing stillwater.

Conditions

On windy days, ponds become easier to read, yet harder to fish, because casting can be a challenge, and seeing rising fish may be next to impossible. But if you think fish are not feeding, think again. The wind creates many areas for trout to feed, similar to streams and rivers. A back eddy may form in a cove where the wind is blowing off a point of land, creating a calm area in the lee behind the point. You will often find a scum line forming in this lee as the wind blows debris and insects into the water and deposits them in a well-defined line just behind and out of the wind-blown water. Fish will often congregate under the debris and feed opportunistically on insects or wounded baitfish being deposited in this area.

Although you can see the debris floating on the surface, just as much and maybe more is often below.

Windy conditions do not hamper trout feeding, in fact they may prompt it. Choose your fishing location carefully.

Feeding activity can take place throughout the water column in these situations, and fishermen should observe the area for rising trout before prospecting below the surface. The fact that many of these debris lines form in the lee of a cove makes spotting rising fish a little easier in windy conditions. Because fish are less spooky in windy, churned-up water you can often get fairly close to a debris line without disturbing feeding fish, which allows you to spot rising fish more effectively and cast shorter distances.

The fish instinctively know that the insects are helpless, so feeding activity is very slow and deliberate. A fisherman concentrating his efforts on a debris line will often see only a subtle, slow rise, or a fin and tail of a feeding trout. Eddies like these can be tricky to cast dry flies into, as the wind may create some current, making this similar to stream fishing. If you find your cast is crossing windswept water as you try to present your fly to a rising fish in a calm spot, and you just can't seem to get the long drift you're looking for, reposition yourself downwind closer to shore and cast into the wind. This not only takes you out of the wind, but also allows you to present your fly with a long drift that eventually works back to your position. As long as your presentation is subtle, accurate, and without drag you may be able to work the fish until you find the right fly and presentation to entice a strike. This is important, as a fly dragged across a rising fish could put the fish down for awhile. The downwind position allows you to work the fly over and over again until you find the right combination to take the fish. If you see no evidence of rising fish, then prospecting the debris line with streamers, nymphs, Woolly Buggers, or leeches can prove deadly.

There is one other important debris line phenomenon. As the wind picks up and waves start to grow, the action of the waves hitting the shoreline and bouncing back into the pond or lake against the wind forms another line of debris that is visible from the lake. These debris lines will often run the entire length of a shoreline. I usually don't bother looking for risers in this situation as they are generally impossible to see unless a fish decides to really thrash the surface looking for a meal. Stick to subsurface flies in this situation, casting beyond the debris and retrieving your fly through or along the edge. This will eventually result in a fish.

I recently had occasion to learn how deadly streamer fishing can be in these situations when fishing Lago Tromen in Argentina's northern Patagonia. Host Ronnie Olsen guided my friend Mike and me to this beautiful lake in the Andes that forms the headwaters of the famed Malleo River. Crystal clear water and a calm day made for tough fishing conditions, but Ronnie knew something we didn't. The wind would blow, as it always does here, and the fishing would get good as soon as it did. As we settled into an early lunch we could feel the wind start to pick up. Ronnie smiled and said "Let's go." Instead of finding a lee shoreline, Ronnie went to the most windy area of the lake. Waves made standing in the boat to cast a challenge, but as we cast toward shore and started to retrieve we could see the distinct line of debris form as the waves hit shore and rebounded back into the lake. Rainbows in the eighteen-to twenty-four-inch range came readily to our olive Woolly Buggers, and fishing was fantastic the rest of the day. As we drifted our last shoreline and I snapped the last few pictures of another of Mike's many rainbows, I realized how important it was to have someone like Ronnie who so graciously allowed us to have this great experience. Without his knowledge of this fishery, we probably would have headed home when the wind picked up.

I have had some twenty- and thirty-fish days fly fishing on stillwaters that were churned up from the wind. Popular fisheries in your area that are normally crowded with anglers are often empty on windy days. Windy conditions can result in some of the year's best fishing if you are able to venture out. You must fish

This angler makes a short cast toward the shoreline where the wind has formed a shady debris line . . .

. . . and takes a nice rainbow as a result!

either from shore or in a stable boat to make this successful, but it's worth it.

Not all prospecting occurs in windy conditions. There are many days when calm waters can be productive, especially in early spring when fish are well dispersed, and again in midsummer when warm surface water temperatures send fish looking for cooler depths, sometimes forty or fifty feet below the surface. Paul Bruun and I share a passion for stillwater lake trout called togue in Canada. They tend to be deepwater fish, hugging bottom most of the year. One of Paul's stillwater techniques involves a deep, slow retrieve of small streamer flies. The trick is feeling the take, often only a very subtle hesitation in your line. You need to be quick

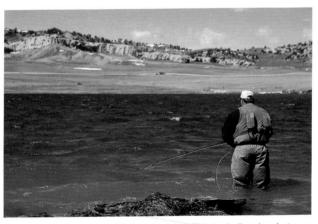

This angler is casting straight into the wind. This is challenging, but most windswept debris will be here on the windward side, as will the trout.

Sometimes casting into the wind can pay off handsomely.

to react in setting the hook. It's easy to overlook the take and not hook the fish, or not even know it was there. Using a Depth Charge line, nine- to twelve-foot leader, and small streamers, Paul lets his line settle to his retrieve depth, usually measured by counting after his line and fly land on the water. It takes some experimentation to know just how deep your fly is. Anchor off shore in twenty-five feet of water (measured with your anchor line) and count as your fly sinks; your fly will eventually hit bottom. Back off on your count and you will be fishing just off bottom. (See sketch.) Another important requirement for this deep-water technique is to feed slack into the water as the line is sinking. If you hold onto the line as it sinks, you act as a pivot or hinge point for your flyline and fly. This causes the fly to swing in an arc back toward you. If you feed slack line into the water as the line and fly is sinking it will allow the line to settle parallel with the bottom, and your retrieve to cover more of the water's bottom than if it had hinged back toward your position when sinking. Add to this a slow retrieve, and your fly will stay just off the bottom longer than if you were to retrieve quickly. Many times fish will take as the fly is swinging up toward the boat, so keep your retrieve steady and be ready for the take all

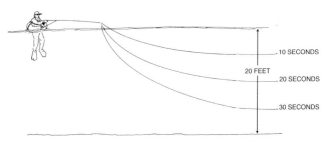

When fishing a sinking line, counting after your fly hits the water will give you an idea how deep it is when you get a strike. Keep fishing to the same count!

the way back to the boat. This technique works well for trout all year in most deep stillwaters.

Retrieves

When prospecting for trout in any weather condition, one becomes proficient at casting and retrieving the fly, over and over again. Change your retrieve and pattern often until you find the right combination for the fish you are seeking. When fishing streamers or nymphs, I may start with a floating line and weighted fly so that I am fishing just below the water's surface, but may change to a full-sinking Depth Charge line that allows me to get deeper more quickly. In these conditions I like to have two rods rigged, one with a floating line and the other with a fast-sinking line.

When fishing nymphs use a longer twelve- to fifteen-foot leader on either a floating or sinking line. The nymphs I fish are always smaller than any streamer I would cast, and so will turn over with the longer leaders. The retrieve is slower and more deliberate than the retrieves used for streamers or leeches, therefore I believe stealth is much more important when fishing nymphs, as the fish has more time to inspect what he is eating.

The retrieve I find most successful is small six- to twelve-inch strips, varying them from slow to fast. The takes can be very subtle, and it is therefore super important to pay attention. There are many fish that eat a nymph and spit it out before the angler even knows that he has had a take.

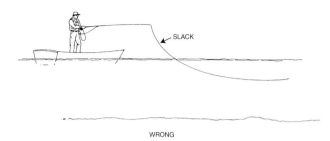

SLACK

WRONG

WRONG: Holding the rod tip high on the retrieve will cause slack and make strikes difficult to detect.

Rule number one, when fishing nymphs with a floating line: Always look at where you think your fly is in the water, and at the same time keep an eye on the end of your fly line. Many times a fish coming for the fly, even though it is subsurface, will make some sort of swirl that you can see from your vantage point. If you don't see the swirl, you should watch for any hesitation, stop, or pull at the end of your fly line that may indicate a fish taking your nymph. Making a long strip or lifting the rod to set the hook when you see any indication of a strike will often result in a hookup. If you think you are missing a lot of fish, increase the speed and length of your retrieve slightly. This will help you feel the strikes, as it keeps a tighter line between you and your fly.

Rule number two: When fishing a full-sinking line you must concentrate on your senses of sight and touch. Your rod should be positioned low to the water so the tip is actually touching the surface as you retrieve. This removes any slack line that would form if

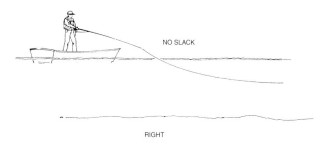

NO SLACK

RIGHT

RIGHT: Holding the rod tip low keeps a straight line between you and the fly, making strike detection easier.

you had your rod a foot or two above the surface of the water. (See sketch.) Any slack will prevent you from feeling those subtle takes during the retrieve. When fishing nymphs on a full-sinking line it is much harder to feel the takes than with a floating line, so your concentration is key to knowing that a fish has just eaten your nymph. As you are retrieving your fly, watch the tip of your rod closely. You will see it fall into a rhythm with your retrieve: It dips the same amount as you pull and releases the same amount when you stop. The combination of looking for a change and feeling a hesitation or pull results in a much more harmonious approach to detecting a strike. Any change in this rhythm should be met with a long strip or a lift of the tip to set the hook. If there is nothing there, go back to your retrieve, but never think that what you felt and saw was not a fish. Always react as if a fish has just eaten your fly. More often than not you will be right. Don't second-guess yourself, because it's too late if you do.

Two Nymphs Are Better Than One

As a variation on the above techniques, two nymphs can be better than one. I have a few good friends in Colorado who, many years ago, taught me never to tie only one nymph on my rig. Monroe Coleman, Mike Clough, and Kevin Gregory are the best nymph fishermen I have ever seen. Each of them has his own unique deadly technique but they all tie on at least two nymphs when fishing.

The key to fishing two nymphs is in how you set up your rig before you cast. The larger or heavier nymph should be at the top closer to your fly line, followed by the smaller nymph trailing sixteen to twenty-four inches behind the first. Tie the dropper directly to the bend of the hook on the heavier fly. This prevents the rig from twisting and spinning as you retrieve it. You will hear fishermen tell you that hooking fish on the top fly is harder because there is a piece of tippet attached to it, and the fish may feel it as they try to take the fly. I think they are right, but I have taken a good number of fish on the upper fly that I would not have caught had it not been there. I also feel that a fish will often see the larger nymph and approach for a look; when confronted with the smaller nymph trailing behind, they quickly eat it. This method simply gives the fish two choices of food, which they would not have had otherwise. It works very well when searching for a pattern the fish will eat. Have I ever taken two fish at once while fishing two nymphs? Rarely, but yes. If they are big, your chances of landing both are slim.

Wayne with a nice rainbow taken on one of his many streamer patterns. Note the fly patch on his vest.

Using Streamers

Never have I witnessed a more dedicated streamer fisherman than my good friend Wayne MacDougall. His vest holds several fly boxes crammed with flies of every color, pattern, shape, and size you could imagine. When most fishermen give it up, Wayne is just getting started, and he produces. His methods include covering all water depths, so he is ready with a Depth Charge as well as a floating fly line. His flies are gaudy creations that include lots of marabou and Krystal Flash in all imaginable colors, although his most successful colors are yellow and black. He varies his retrieves along with the depth, until he hits on a combination that works. I have seen few occasions when Wayne is not catching fish using his deadly techniques.

I recall a memorable occasion where several of us, including Wayne, had a tremendous hatch of blue-winged olives (BWO) coming off a stillwater on a calm evening. Trout were readily sipping duns that sat on the water's surface, but trying to catch a trout seemed an impossible challenge. I had covered rises for an hour with nary a bite, while Wayne was reeling in his fourth fish. Last I knew he was fishing a #20 BWO trying to trick these fish into eating, so as he brought in his fourth fish I thought he had found the right combination to take these finicky trout. But as I gathered the courage to ask, I found his deadly fly was a #2 black marabou creation he had whipped up.

When fishing streamers, Woolly Buggers, and leeches, use slightly shorter leaders. I recommend a longer twelve-foot leader on a floating line and a shorter nine-foot (seven-and-a-half-foot if you are trying to stay tight to bottom) leader on full-sinking lines. Unlike the nymph fishing we discussed above, the takes are aggressive and quick, so 2X or 3X leaders should be used, especially when fishing in windy conditions. In lakes and ponds with large eight-pounds-plus fish, a 0X or 1X leader is not too big. Be ready for the yank of a lifetime when you least expect it. When retrieving flies on either floating or sinking lines use long, full strips with varying rates of speed. I often find trout turn on to very fast, long strips of a Woolly Bugger or leech, and here the strikes are the most vicious of all. This is one of the most successful prospecting techniques going, as you can cover a lot of water quickly and efficiently.

Baitfish can get disoriented or separated from their schools in windy situations, so trout are on the lookout for an imitation that looks like a lost soldier. When fishing streamers that are imitating baitfish, use lighter 3X to 4X leaders to start. To make the fly act like a wounded baitfish, make a few quick strips, stop, then two or three longer strips, then stop. Change it up so your retrieve is not monotonous. Takes will range from the subtle to the explosive so you need to be ready for

Tom Rosenbauer took this monster landlocked salmon while fishing a New York stillwater in October. The fish chased the streamer several times before hitting. (Tom Rosenbauer photo)

either. In the fall when fishing for Northeast landlocked salmon on lakes and ponds, where fish are more likely to take small attractor streamers slowly stripped, the takes are more similar to those you get when fishing nymphs. Watch for swirling fish. Fish that make a pass at the fly but do not eat it will often take a different pattern presented to them. I have found that if a fish comes up and looks a couple times at a pattern and then disappears it will often come back and eat a different pattern presented as a follow-up. Fish will invariably come back and investigate until they see something that triggers the take. So quickly change your fly and recast to the same area, and keep doing this until he takes.

Using Dry Flies

As deadly and persistent as Wayne is with streamers, my Dad (Chuck) is the same with his dry-fly fishing. My Dad has been a relentless dry-fly fisherman for years. He just really hates to take off a dry fly, and would rather prospect with drys than go to a nymph or streamer, even if someone is catching a bunch of fish on them. He likes the challenge of fishing drys, and will figure it out. In the end he catches fish, a lot of fish. He is patient and works to put together the same combination of pattern, size, color, and presentation that Wayne has worked out with his streamers. His relentless pursuit of trout on dry flies has given me insight into successful techniques that take trout.

Of all the fishing experiences I have been able to share with my Dad, the one involving dry-fly fishing that sticks most in my mind took place on Pierce Pond in Maine in the early 1980s. We had, for a number of years, tented in a remote cove (called the Scott Paper site) for a week in early July in anticipation of the giant *Hexagenia limbata* mayfly hatch that was prolific on this pond. I always fished floating nymphs early in the hatch before the fish started to rise. I could occasionally get fish to take a nymph stripped slowly just under the surface, but never fished drys this early on. There were no flies on the surface so logically why would I want to prospect with one? Dad tied on a large Black Wulff pattern we had tied during the day and started prospecting. Patiently casting and letting his fly sit on the water, he soon had an aggressive take from a big brook trout. Bringing the fish to the canoe, I could see that it was one of the bigger trout I had ever seen on Pierce Pond. We landed the fish, measured it at twenty-one inches, and released it. It didn't stop there, and Dad proceeded to have the best single night of prospecting for trout that I have ever seen. One trout measured twenty-five inches in length and must have weighed all of eight pounds. He still glows when we talk about that evening. It has been a valuable reminder of the success you can have prospecting with drys.

On really calm days I will often prospect with dry flies close to shore or in areas where deepwater shoals rise to within a couple of feet of the surface. You'll be surprised how many fish will come to a dry fly dropped within a few feet of their position. In these situations it is important to read the water around you.

A big mayfly and its dry-fly imitation. On calm days, prospecting near shore with a dry fly is often an effective strategy. (*Tom Rosenbauer photo*)

Fish looking for food along these shorelines are feeding opportunistically subsurface, close to shore, and on the surface. They spot a fly in their path and rise to eat it as they continue on their way looking for more.

Work the shorelines in these situations, making a few casts in one area, then move on. Once you catch a fish, concentrate some time and effort in the area before moving on. You will often find a shoal, point, or section of shoreline where fish are feeding more readily than in other areas. Spend some time in such spots, as different fish will come in and out in search of food.

On stillwater a dry fly should be cast and left for some time before picking it up to recast. I have seen too many anglers who do not have the patience to leave a fly in one spot long enough. They seem to think they need to keep the fly in the air or strip it back to get fish to strike. Remember that the fish are moving and may not instantly take your offering. There are several tricks to the cast-and-wait method that you should be aware of. Most important is the relationship of your fly line to the fly on the water. You will find that after you cast a dry fly on stillwater things don't stay exactly the same until you pick up your line for a recast. You must constantly tend your line to keep slack from forming between you and your fly. If you are in a moving canoe or float tube, you will find that a belly or arc forms between you and the fly, making it hard to set the hook. It's pretty exciting to see a fish you didn't anticipate come up and gulp your offering, so be ready.

ANTICIPATING A HATCH

While prospecting on stillwater, something you observe while fishing will usually be a key to some later activity that will increase your fishing opportunities. Careful observation of the areas you are prospecting will often reveal a subsurface swirl, the remains of nymph cases floating in the water or gathered along shorelines, or flies in the trees.

In any stillwater the majority of hatching or emerging activity will take place in the shallows. Because sunlight and water temperatures are important to insect life, areas with rocky points, shallow silty coves, overhanging trees, undercut banks, weedy shorelines, and areas with subsurface structure like sunken logs or half-submerged fallen trees may create the conditions for a hatch you will see later today, or tomorrow. A sure sign that a specific cove or section of a stillwater is experiencing a hatch is nymph cases floating in the water or washed up on shore. These cases are left as nymphs emerge to become flying adults. By either swimming or floating to the surface they shed their outer skins and emerge like a butterfly from a cocoon, leaving an empty hull floating in the surface layer. The insects are most vulnerable during this emerging phase, drawing fish to feed during the transformation. If you are there right after a hatch you may find these cases still floating in the area where they emerged. If you find cases later in the day, they have usually been carried closer to shorelines with the wind and are bunched together in a debris field.

These nymph cases can unlock a door to some intense fishing activity during the right time of day. If you are just arriving at a stillwater for the first time or the trip is just getting started, make it a point to search windward shorelines or coves for these remains during your day on the water. If you have done your entomology homework you will be able to determine whether the cases are from caddis, mayflies, stoneflies, midges, or other insects that have hatched.

The length and width of the case also gives you an idea of the fly size you should start with. If there is no apparent emerging activity, start with a nymph resembling the remains you have found. Fish it below the water's surface at varying depths. Chances are the nymph cases you have discovered along the shore represent an increase in the activity of a particular species.

I love to fish the *Hexagenia* hatch in the Northeast. I know from years of fishing this hatch that it occurs at night from the last week of June into the first week of July. I also know that certain coves are better than others. If I have only a day to fish this hatch (I would rather stay a week), I will arrive early and survey coves that have silt bottoms, looking for last night's cases bunched up along the shore. Once I have found an area with cases, chances are I can count on the hatch to take place again tonight in this same area. I will anchor or stake out an area close to where I think the highest activity will take place, and will immediately start to prospect with large *Hex* nymphs. I know these nymphs are in the area and if they are emerging they must be in a state of increased activity, drawing the fish. As evening approaches I will switch from fishing nymphs deep to fishing nymphs just under the surface, as I expect the real ones will be making their way up to emerge. And just at dark, and hopefully just

An early *Hexagenia limbata* mayfly, a sure sign of what's to come in the evening.

before the major hatch, I fish a dry-fly in hopes of taking a trophy.

Keeping an eye skyward will often show flies that may be coming off intermittently. An occasional rise on stillwater should be enough to make you look in the air to see what may be emerging. This early indicator to a potential hatch can result in an opportunity for you to get an early start on some great fishing action.

Observation is key to anticipating what is going to happen, and I believe that anytime you fish stillwater you should be trying to predict what might happen next.

FISHING THE HATCH

When a hatch starts, I have seen even the best fishermen fumble, bumble, and grumble their way through wind knots, tangles, and misguided casts. Keen observation is very important both before the hatch occurs and again after it starts. Fish are often seen swirling subsurface at emerging nymphs. Often this is your clue of a hatch about to come.

You should fish floating lines during a hatch. Pick a color that is bright enough to see during the day, but that also can be seen easily in dimming light. Yellow is a good color for both situations. Bright colors like orange are great during the day, but become a challenge to see in dimming light.

Leader length and tippet size depends on the flies you will be using during the hatch. Large wind-resistant drys in #6 to #8 call for seven-and-a-half- to nine-foot leaders in with 2X to 3X tippets. Any longer or finer

Shaking the trees along the shoreline produced a cloud of caddisflies. A couple of hours later, trout were rising to the egg-laying adults.

and the leader will twist during casting. If this happens at dark just as the hatch is reaching its peak you may find yourself in quite a mess. Worse yet, you usually do not see it happen until it gets so bad you have to start over again. Flies in the normal #10 to #16 range can be cast with a nine- to twelve-foot leader and tippets in the 4X to 5X category. Flies smaller than #16 need a leader of twelve-feet or longer and tippets of 6X or 7X. Dress your dry flies with a floatant before casting them; this keeps your fly on top for awhile before you have to pick up and recast. If fishing extremely calm water, I like to use fluorocarbon tippet, as it breaks the surface tension of water and sinks slightly. A commercial preparation called Mud can be applied to nylon tippets so they also break the surface tension. In very calm water, your tippet and leader close to the fly will be just below the surface, thereby avoiding any shadows made by dimples as your leader sits in the film. The shadows make your fly, and the area around it, look suspicious to cruising trout. They will often turn away from your fly if this happens. This is one reason I like to locate spots that have a slight riffle when fishing drys. The small waves or riffles help hide the leader and tippet, so fish are less likely to spook.

Stillwater trout do not rise in the same place over and over again. They cruise, and you may find one particular fish working an area back and forth, but covering large sections of stillwater looking for insects. When a hatch reaches its peak, you will find the fish with the insects. If only one cove has emerging mayflies, there will be more fish here than anywhere else on the pond. This is another good reason to do your pre-hatch homework.

Large western brown and rainbow trout, and eastern brook trout, are normally lone cruisers. As a hatch gets started they can be seen rising, and a few seconds later they rise again some distance away. This usually gives you an indication of which way the fish is moving. A cast aimed to intercept the fish will often result in a rise to your fly. Eastern brookies seem to move consistently in a straight line, and are more predictable than western browns and rainbows. Nonetheless it is possible to get the fly in the area of a brown's or rainbow's next rise if you spend some time watching them.

In the Northeast, landlocked salmon will often move together in schools to feed during a hatch. Activity is much more erratic as the school moves through the area, and picking a single fish is next to impossible. A cast in the middle of the area where activity is highest will often be met with an aggressive rise due to competition from neighboring fish. In addition, I have seen trout in a given size class school together on stillwater both in the East and West, exhibiting this same behavior.

If the hatch is sporadic yet consistent, fishing will often be much better than if the hatch is a full-blown whiteout. When fish rise close to you, casting your fly to cover the rise will sometimes bring the fish back up in the same spot to take your fly. Get your fly quickly to the rise ring before the fish moves away. If fish are consistently rising all around you, disregard them, be patient, and wait for a fish to move to your fly. Trying to cover all the rings in the middle of a good hatch will have your fly in the air more than on the water. Remember also that when fishing from a boat or float tube, chasing rising fish will only result in chasing more rising fish. Stay put, let the area around you settle down, and trust that the fish will move in to feed. They will come to you if you have the patience.

When presenting your dry fly on stillwater, unlike with nymphs and streamers, you seldom strip your fly back. With drys, leave your fly on the water and wait. Don't be impatient. Many anglers cast, let their fly land on the water, and if not met with an immediate take they pick up and cast again. Two things happen when an angler does this: The action of lifting the line off the water over and over will eventually spook most of the fish around you, and they'll stay outside of the circle of your longest cast. Be patient, cast your dry fly, leave it, and watch it.

You *will* have to do some line management when fishing drys. As you watch your fly on the water it appears to be staying in one place, but it isn't. If the wind is moving directly away from you, the fly line will usually stay fairly tight, requiring little management. Usually in this situation I find that the fly sinking is more of a problem than managing slack line. If the fly sinks, bring it in, dry it off, and recast.

More often than not you will see slack forming in your fly line that needs to be taken in so that you have a direct connection to your fly in the event of a strike. Take in only enough line to keep the slack from forming; do not strip in so much that you start moving your fly. When the fly gets fairly close to you, pick it up and recast to another area. Fan your casts around to cover the water. If you do this, you will not be spooking fish

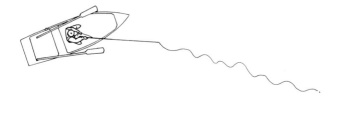

WRONG

WRONG: Slack in the line will prevent you from having a direct connection with the dry fly in the event of a strike.

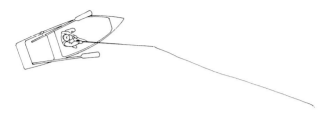

RIGHT: Take in enough line to keep slack from forming, but do not strip in so much that you actually move the fly, which should remain still on the surface.

by constantly picking up line off the water, and you will have more fish cruise in close to you. I have had fish take the fly within a couple of feet of the boat, so don't think you have to have the fly sixty feet away. Remember, the trout are cruising, so less wriggling and more patience will pay off.

In the midst of a heavy hatch when it appears to be raining flies, or the water's surface looks as if it has a blanket of insects covering every square inch, you will probably need to change your tactics. During these times I have had fish spend way too much time examining my fly, then pass on it with a swirl just to let me know they were looking. Going to a different size fly, either bigger or smaller, or maybe a caddis instead of a mayfly, is the ticket to breaking the ice. Something a little different will often make them rise without hesitation, while mimicking the hatch would have gotten you nothing.

TECHNIQUES AND STRATEGIES

SIGHT-FISHING FOR TROPHY TROUT

When conditions are just right, sight-fishing for cruising trout is like hunting for big bonefish in the Bahamas. It will take some patience and practice, but the thrill of watching a trout cruise the shore, see your fly, and then take it brings a new level of excitement for the stillwater angler. I love sight-fishing for trout, but weather, light conditions, shorelines, fish movement, and more need to be in your favor before you go prowling the shorelines in search of a trout.

There are three methods of stillwater trout fishing that could be called sight-fishing: Shoreline wading in search of cruising trout, sight-fishing for weed bed trout that are either sipping insects or looking for scuds and midges, and shallow cove sight-fishing from a boat. For the most part, these three situations cover the majority of your stillwater sight-fishing opportunities. In all of these situations you should fish a floating line. Leaders of nine-feet minimum and preferably twelve-feet or longer should be used in all sight-fishing situations. The diameter of your tippet will range from 4X for larger nymphs to 7X for midges in weed beds.

Lee Wulff once told me that if a fish had refused his fly, before he changed it he always dropped down one tippet size first. I have never forgotten that bit of advice and now pass it on to you. Usually if you are getting refusals the fish is attracted by your fly but is turning off because of something else he sees just before he eats it. A heavy tippet sometimes gives the fly

Clear days with light winds offer the best sight-fishing opportunities.
This can be like stalking bonefish on a tropical flat.

a stiff look, or the fish can see it in really clear water.
So try a finer tippet before changing your fly.

Before we start talking about the various opportunities for sight-fishing, I need to mention that in sight-fishing more than anywhere else, a good pair of polarized sunglasses is a must-have item. Amber or copper lenses are my choice for sight-fishing. Amber is best in all conditions, but I have found that copper outperforms amber in low-light situations. I like carrying both, but if you have to choose one color I would recommend a good pair of amber polarized sunglasses.

Cruisin' for a Bruisin'

Clear days with low winds offer the best sight-fishing opportunities. Do a little homework before jumping into the pond, though. The sun will be your best friend when sight-fishing, but it can turn into your enemy if you are not paying attention to its relation to you and your quarry. The best hours for sight-fishing are from midmorning through late afternoon. Depending on the season, these hours range from long in midsummer to only a few hours in late fall or winter. It is an advantage to have the sun somewhere behind you, so locate a shoreline where the sun will be at your back. It does not have to be directly behind you but it should be in a position that allows you to see into the water for the greatest distance. If the sun quarters off one shoulder or another it should be fine.

Generally speaking, in the United States, where the sun rises in the east and sets in the west, here is a good rule of thumb that you can use to find good shorelines for sight-fishing at various times of the day:

- In early morning, when light just starts to get strong enough so you can see into the water, south shorelines moving west, north shorelines moving west, and east shorelines moving north will be your best bets.
- At high noon, look for south shorelines moving either east or west, or east and west shorelines moving north. (See sketch.)
- As the sun sets, fish north or south shorelines moving east, or west shorelines moving north.

After sun position, wind direction is the second order of business when looking for a shoreline to wade. Keep in mind that you have several options of shore-

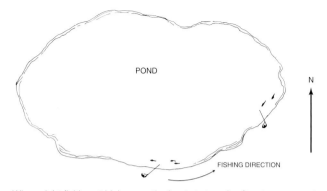

When sight-fishing at high noon, the best strategy is often to move east along the south shoreline. But keep the wind in mind as well.

lines to fish depending on the time of day. If it is high noon and you have a strong wind coming from the northeast, the east shoreline moving north would be a good bet. It will be slightly out of the wind and will keep your line away from you if you're a right-handed caster. Consider this before hiking to a fishing spot.

Obviously, the shoreline of the pond you are fishing must have other important attributes in order to sight-fish. You must be able to see bottom along the shoreline you are fishing. The shoreline needs to be wadable, with firm footing for a long distance. A shoreline that does not drop-off quickly, yet allows you to see into waist-deep water easily, is prime. The bottom should be fairly light colored and rocky, with stretches of hard sandy areas to make spotting fish a little easier. The water must be relatively clear, as sight-fishing in churned-up water just does not work.

Sight-fishing can produce some great catches, like this trophy rainbow.

Normally, when you are sight-fishing a long rocky shoreline, like that on Duck Lake in Glacier National Park, fish cruise and feed on anything that strays into their path. On occasion they may come up for dry flies, but more often than not they are feeding on nymphs when cruising shorelines. I like to tie on a No. 12 or 14 nymph to start my sight-fishing. If I am fishing deeper water (twenty-four to thirty-six inches) a beadhead mayfly or weighted scud pattern that will sink fairly quickly and get to the fish's cruising level, would be my choice. In shallower water, use the same patterns without beads, epoxy-back mayfly nymphs, soft-hackle caddis, or other nymphs that simulate insects found in the pond you are fishing.

Walk the shoreline slowly in search of your first fish. Trout are not always easy to spot. I have spent many days with anglers who are not familiar with spotting fish, even when wearing the best sunglasses. Some people pick it up very quickly while others don't see the fish until they are too close for a decent cast or presentation. Keep practicing! The key is to look for a shadow or a movement that is not attached to the bottom. Don't worry about casting to what you thought was a trout but turned out to be a rock. The situation will soon improve. When it all comes together you will be spotting fish at thirty or forty yards, with plenty of time to get your knees to stop shaking and make your cast.

On lakes like Duck Lake, where you can spend a morning working a single shoreline, fish over ten pounds are not uncommon. Your cast should land far enough in front of the fish so the fly will be at his level when he gets to it. If you lead him too much, the fish can easily change direction, and you will have to cast again to get back in front of the fish. Many factors must be considered: How fast is the fish moving? How deep is it? Is it swimming erratically or does it seem to be cruising in a straight line? Make your own calculations; each situation will be different. I have seen shallow cruisers in a foot of water with their noses in the rocks looking for nymphs, so I had to put a fly a couple of inches from their snouts, while deepwater trout may move twenty feet out of their way for a poorly presented fly. Don't cast over their backs, or let the fly land on top of their heads, that much I can tell you for sure!

When you make the right cast, the fish will react to your offering, and now comes the next critical step in catching it. When fishing nymphs I have found that free-falling nymphs work better than nymphs stripped

Sight-fishing can be difficult, but the rewards can make the challenge worthwhile.

back. Trout see the nymph falling, move toward it, and almost always turn slightly to eat. You need to meet this with either a lift of the rod or a strip strike, as more often than not you will not feel the take, but will only see it. Although I utilize strip strikes for bonefishing or tarpon fishing, I find it more difficult when fishing stillwater. Stillwater anglers like Tom Rosenbauer and Marty Cecil utilize a strip strike once the fish takes the fly. To make a strip strike, keep your rod pointing at the fish with the tip low, almost touching the water. As the fish takes the fly, a long strip will often be met with the resistance of the fish on the other end. If not, your fly, still in front of the fish, will often be pursued and eaten. In either case, if you wait to feel the fish on the end of your line it is too late, as it has had time to spit out the fly and move off.

As you move slowly and look for cruising trout you will find some areas with little or no activity and others where every few feet you have another trout come along. If you go through a hot spot, reel in, go back to where you started, and work this area again, or look for the next area along the shoreline that has the same attributes as the one just fished. Usually a point of land will mark an area of increased activity, as trout tend to bounce off points. Also food is deposited more readily in these areas. Be on the alert for patterns and areas of increased activity.

Sometimes you find trout cruising high up in the water, looking for dry flies on the surface, sipping in whatever happens to be in their path. Changing to a dry in these situations is recommended if you have seen fish hover close to the surface, or have spotted a good bit of rising activity down the shoreline. Once you have seen the fish and marked his rising activity, cast your fly to intercept him. Watch the fish closely as he approaches your fly and don't get overly excited and pull the fly away from him. It's hard to do, but if all goes well the fish will inhale your fly and turn away with fly in mouth. Lift your rod to set the hook.

You will have a higher success rate hooking stillwater trout if you can wait until the fish turns and starts back down with your fly. It's just a split second but makes a huge difference in hookup rate.

Midge Cruisers and Weed Bed Sippers

In this section I'll focus on trout that are found cruising and feeding selectively on smaller nymphs. These trout are not the free-ranging cruisers discussed above but rather are found in shallow, weedy, stillwater areas. They often stay in one small area, circling or moving back and forth along a shoreline in a repetitive feeding pattern. I consider these trout to be the most difficult fish to take on a fly, for several reasons: They are usually really focused on a specific nymph, in many cases swimming with their mouths open taking in clusters of midges that have been blown in large groups onto the water's surface. They are the most erratic of feeders and the hardest to figure out in terms of where they are going next. And they are usually found in areas of dense weed growth, so once you hook them the challenge begins all over again as they put their heads down and bury themselves in the weeds.

Use tippets or leaders in the 5X to 7X range for this fishing. If using scuds you may be able to get away with 5X, but for midge larvae or nymphs in the No. 18 to 24 range use tippets in sizes 6X or 7X.

I highly recommend fluorocarbon leader or tippet material for this fishing. You can often get away with one tippet size larger when using it, and thus gain an advantage when the fight begins, but also this fishing is usually in shallow, calm water, where a material that blends in or disappears in the water becomes a great stealth advantage. I prefer twelve-foot knotless tapered leaders here as a minimum length.

This fishing is found in smaller stillwaters, or in small areas of big stillwaters. Wading may or may not be an option, as weed beds may be so heavy near shore that you will need to be in a boat or float tube fishing the outside edges of the weeds. In others you will see areas between the weeds and shore where cruising fish can be found. I have found that on smaller stillwaters fishing from shore is usually a good bet, whereas small areas on large stillwaters where weed beds are found are often better fished from a tube or boat.

Remember that the sun position and wind direction are factors to consider in deciding where you will start fishing. Once you have done that, standing back from shore and observing the area you are fishing will often reveal fish that are within a couple of feet of shore, moving slowly down the shoreline looking for their next meal. Take some time to watch these fish. When do they eat? Are they rooting around the bottom? Are they sipping off the top? If you spend time watching the trout before casting, your success rate will increase.

These trout may be taking small flies, often not even apparent to you. If the trout are cruising and rooting the bottom, try a Brassy, small glass beadhead midge pupa, or another slow-sinking nymph in a No. 18 or 20. You will need to use at least a 6X to start, but before changing flies, if you have no interest from the trout, try going to 7X first. If they are sipping off the top and seem to be feeding just subsurface, tying on two nymphs can often be a good bet. A small midge dry at the top followed by an emerger or nymph about sixteen to twenty inches back can be a deadly presentation in these situations. You may have to cast more line on shore than in the water. There is a small spring creek in my yard that flows into a small stillwater area the size of large bathtub. Anyone walking within thirty feet of this pool sees nothing but riffles as small brook trout take cover under a large rock that sits at the head of the pool. I occasionally try my luck casting to these wary trout, and in order to catch one I need to position myself about forty feet from the pool, and thirty-seven feet of line lands on the grass. Some stillwater situations demand this same technique. When presenting a fly this way you cannot strip line back in or you will get caught on everything between you and the water. You must lift the line straight up and out of the grass and rocks. If all goes as planned you can cast back into the area for another try at the trout you have your eye on. If all does not go as planned you will get your hook caught on a blade of grass or the only stick between you and your fish. It's decision time: Break it off, or go and get it? If the trout is still in casting range and I expect it will be cruising a small area for a while, I'll break it off and tie a new fly on. I hate to leave fish to look for other fish I may or may not find. A hookup on the other hand, carries a whole different set of rules.

If the cast is rewarded by a trout on the end of your line, the work has just begun. I said earlier that trout found in weedy areas require special care. You *will* lose fish. Don't be disappointed, the best anglers in the world lose them too. But you can improve your odds. Keep your rod high, I mean really high. Reach up as far as you can over your head and leave your rod there. The fish will head for the weeds, and the high rod angle makes the fish work hard to get there. If he makes it and appears to be caught up don't panic, but keep steady pressure on. Often the fish will back very slowly out of the weeds and you can begin the battle again. In the event the fish seems to be stuck and not moving, release all pressure on the fish and let him think he has gotten off. The fish will often back out of the weeds on his own, allowing you to bring the line tight on a surprised trout and resume the battle. It is a real thrill when the trout finally comes to net, covered in the debris of the weedy bottom.

Fishing the weeds can be very effective, especially with a float tube.

Sight-fishing from a boat for cruising trout along weed beds that lie in deeper water is a slightly different game. Float tube or canoe sight-fishing is not easy, and all conditions must be perfect for this to be successful, as your low angle to the water is poor for spotting fish. I would recommend a boat that you can stand in for sight-fishing. You will be higher off the water at a much better angle for spotting fish.

Stillwaters that have coves or shorelines lined with weed beds will bring trout from deepwater sections in to feed. They move into weedy areas and cruise for dislodged or swimming nymphs or scuds, and may opportunistically rise to a fly during this activity. Watch the fish as it feeds along its cruise path. Is the fish cruising high or low in the water column? If the fish is high up in the water, just under the surface, I will often fish a small dry and a dropper. A midge dry-fly with a small midge dropper eighteen to twenty-four inches behind, or a caddis with a scud dropper are two combinations to try. Giving the trout a choice helps you to narrow down what they are feeding on and gives you twice the chance to catch them. If fishing clearwater ponds try not to cast too close as this often spooks the fish. A cast ten feet away on the same line that the trout is cruising will not spook the fish, and I have seen trout go well out of their way to take a fly presented some distance from their actual location. If the fish swims in the vicinity of the fly and refuses it, wait for him to cruise well past your fly before picking it up to recast. He may not have seen your first presentation, and a second or even a third cast may be needed to catch him.

Shallow Cove Sight-Fishing

There are times when you will find fish just cruising in shallow bays and coves looking for a meal. I have found few eastern stillwaters that have good sight-fishing for fish cruising in the shallows, but western stillwater opportunities abound. I have learned a lot by fishing with western anglers who have made fly fishing stillwaters their favorite pastime.

On Trapper's Lake outside of Meeker, Colorado I have had the opportunity to fish for cruisers that could be seen easily a hundred feet away coming into shallow coves looking for a meal. My son Brian, a well-seasoned Colorado fishing guide and stillwater angler, turned me on to the Trapper's Lake fishery a couple of years ago. On this special trip we encountered a great *Callibaetis* mayfly hatch in a shallow silty cove across

Western stillwaters offer abundant opportunities for sight-fishing in shallow coves.

the lake from our access site. From a distance we could see an occasional rise and when we got closer we found trout cruising the bay eating both nymphs and emerging mayflies. There was a constant stream of cutthroats and rainbows moving in and out of the cove, and we found the fish were happy taking either the nymph or a low-riding emerger. We sat anchored up in this cove for a few hours of nonstop dry-fly fishing, all the while seeing each fish we cast to.

In these situations I have found that fish tend to move into a cove mainly from one specific direction. Whether it is the contour of the bottom or unseen currents that cause the fish to cruise in a set pattern and rhythm, I don't know. But you will find, after awhile, that there is a pattern to their approach and you will start looking toward the same area for cruising trout to enter your field of vision. I like to cast well in front of these cruisers, so as not to spook them, but into their path so that they will swim by my fly. Long, twelve- to fifteen-foot leaders are an advantage in this situation and will help keep fish from spooking as the fly lands on the water. Takes are subtle, slow, and deliberate, so don't get overly excited as the fish approaches your fly. Wait until he eats it before yelling and screaming.

FISHING FRY BASHES

"Oh yeah, we fish fry bashes in late summer or early fall. You wouldn't believe the brook trout we catch," Jeff said with excitement as evening approached on King and Bartlett Pond. Jeff Charles, head guide and manager of King and Bartlett Sporting Camps in Maine, has discovered a connection between schooled-up bait along the shorelines and a trouting opportunity I had often overlooked. Although I had observed and fished to schooled-up bait pods in late summer and early fall, Jeff had observed that these baitfish schools were the result of several trout corralling bait toward shore and then bashing the schooled bait, thus Jeff's term "fry bash." (This term may have its origins in England, according to well-known author Tom Rosenbauer.) The result of this bashing is often dozens of stunned, half-alive baitfish that become easy targets for feeding trout.

The first sign of this activity will often be the slight dimpling of baitfish along shore as they are being schooled up. Occasionally you will see an aggressive splash along the shoreline. Investigating this activity is worth it. In these situations, fishing a baitfish imitation that exactly imitates the schooled-up bait is key. A Black-Nosed Dace, Muddler Minnow, or Grey Ghost streamer would be my first choice.

If fishing to the dimpling of bait along the shore, cast your streamer to one side of the pod, not directly into it. Trout often cruise the edges of the pod, and may not take a streamer cast into the middle. A baitfish that strays outside the pod will often be hit as trout prepare to bash the school. If trout are actually crashing bait, cast your streamer directly into the fray. Let it settle, twitch it once, and let it sit still again. Try to make it look like a stunned bait. Trout sweeping back through will often take your streamer as it settles toward bottom, so be ready.

Marabou Muddler

0   1

Mickey Finn

0   1

Streamers and Muddlers are effective patterns for fishing a fry bash.

BEAVER POND TROUT

Some of my most memorable stillwater experiences have been on small beaver ponds scattered throughout the western and eastern United States. Often overlooked by many fishermen, these little gems can be both a challenging and rewarding experience. I met my wife Deb while fishing a small beaver pond flowage in Rocky Mountain National Park, so my fond memories encompass more than the trout I caught, but also the catch of my life. Even before I met my wife I was hooked on beaver ponds as my father took my brother and me to the far reaches of the headwaters of Bemis Stream in the Rangeley Lakes region of Maine. I can remember days when trout came to net one after another, some as large as twelve inches, a good trout on any beaver pond. In more recent years Tom Rosenbauer, who shares a love for beaver pond fly fishing, has been both a partner and a teacher. Tom observes beaver ponds in New England through the winter months in search of the springs that feed them. The springs, often unfrozen in winter, will be key in the summer as trout congregate there in search of cooler water temperatures.

Beaver pond trout are often easy prey for a well-presented dry fly. They do not see many fishermen so they are often voracious feeders, eating almost anything presented. I have been to many small, remote beaver dams that offer fishing for small trout in the six- to nine-inch class, where every cast will be rewarded by a trout hitting your fly. Whether fishing a dry, nymph, or streamer, it appears you can do no wrong. In still others, one good six-inch fish will be the fish of the day.

A more humbling experience is fishing to the large trout that inhabit some beaver dams in the West. Bob Auger, for many years the riverkeeper on DePuy Spring Creek in Paradise Valley, Montana, was one of the best technical fishermen I ever fished with. Before the floods of the Yellowstone wiped out most of DePuy Creek in the mid 1990s, there was a large beaver dam in the lower reaches of the creek that everyone went around in order to fish the lower creek before it emptied into the Yellowstone River. Bob brought Tom and me to this beaver dam in the early 1990s and proceeded to show us the trout that everyone was passing up. Fishing an Orvis One-Weight rod and light tippet, Bob cast and landed a five-pound brown that looked as though it had never been caught. It looked easy, as trout slowly sipped midges off the pond's surface. Tom and I soon found that imitation and presentation were key to getting one of these finicky trout to take our offerings. Once a fish was hooked, the beaver pond offered its challenges in the downed timber that had been flooded in the making of the pond. It took us a while to land a trout, but the fishing was spectacular, with no pressure from other fishermen. This is not an uncommon experience when fishing spring-fed beaver ponds of the West.

PART FOUR

ENTOMOLOGY

Ponds with consistent water depths will often have well-dispersed insect activity and you may find feeding fish anywhere and everywhere. In other still-waters, a specific cove, a shoreline, a certain time of year, or a host of other variables will be the key to unlocking the insect mystery and to catching trout. Your ability to locate these areas, identify species of insects, and match the hatch will allow you to fish these areas successfully. A brief discussion of important stillwater insects, where they're likely to be found, what they look like, and which patterns you should need will help you get started. Each type of insect has its unique characteristics. The more you know about them the more successful you will be.

CADDISFLIES

With over 900 different species in the United States, caddis are widely distributed and second in abundance only to midges. Sizes of these insects vary from a couple of millimeters to over an inch in length, and their normal life cycle is generally a year, although some species can emerge twice in a year and yet others live two years before emerging. As larvae many species construct cases around themselves using bits of vegetation, sticks, or sand and can easily be identified

Adult caddisflies gather in great numbers on leaves along bushy shore-lines. Trout often lie in wait for them to fall into the water.

crawling along the bottom in these forms. Just prior to emerging the nymphs go through a pupal phase transformation, developing oarlike legs used to swim to the surface when emerging. Some species paddle to the surface quickly and then swim to the shore where they crawl out to dry off and fly to neighboring bushes as adults. This swimming action brings about some great feeding activity as caddis make their way toward shore.

As adults, caddis will often be seen in great numbers along bushy shorelines. A little wind or a shake of the bushes along the shoreline will often result in an amazing cloud of insects taking flight. Trout can often be found cruising tight to shore waiting for a good wind to blow the adults from their bushy perch onto the water's surface where they can be eaten. So when caddis are numerous along the shorelines keep an eye open for trout close to shore. A recent trip to Labrador for brook trout resulted in the biggest fish of the trip being taken on caddis drifted within a few inches of the shorelines. Caddis adults were abundant in the shoreline trees and bushes, and trout were cruising in wait of the unsuspecting adult caddis that dropped onto the water's surface. This activity often goes undetected unless you are keenly aware of it.

Caddis that are getting ready to drop their eggs, or oviposit, will skitter above the water's surface, usually en masse, as evening approaches. Leaving their leafy hiding places, caddis will suddenly be seen everywhere, giving the appearance of a migration of flies. Caddis will oviposit by dipping down repeatedly into the water, depositing eggs on surface vegetation, or by crawling below the water's surface to attach eggs to the bottom. Trout will feed on caddis either in the surface film or below the surface during this time. Not all caddis ovipositing activity takes place in the evening. I have found some good activity of small black caddis during daylight hours. This can bring about some great midday opportunities during the summer months. While many anglers take the hotter middle-of-the-day hours off, I have had some great midday experiences with dry flies while having the water to myself. The small black caddis is active most of the day, and if you can get out of the wind or into a cove or lee shoreline that has just a slight riffle you'll have great sport. I like a slight riffle to help hide any flaws in my casting, and so my leader and tippet knots are not quite as evident as they would be on calm water. Twitching your fly slightly to imitate the skittering caddis will often entice a take. Patience is the name of the game here. Don't chase the rise rings, stay in one place, settle yourself down, and be persistent. Fish are cruising and will eventually come to you. Chasing them usually just spooks them.

Fish these and other caddis on a nine-foot to twelve-foot leader. The longer the better, as the further your fly is from the tip of your fly line, the better your chance of a strike. There are two ways to fish the dry flies: Dead-drifting an imitation patiently in wait for a passing fish, or twitching one back to imitate the skittering female. Patterns fished close to shore where fish are cruising for caddis falling from shoreline trees should be fished mostly on a dead drift. I may occasionally twitch the pattern to give it a little life, but I have found that the fish are apt to take these patterns when they are still. A twitched fly will often get the fish's attention. Once this happens, the dead-drift fly will often get the strike. Because fish cruising the shore for fallen caddis tend to rise slowly for their quarry, a twitched fly will often get a close inspection, but the fish will turn off at the last second, refusing the offering. Caddis fished in deeper water where they are found skittering over the surface should be fished with some movement. As I said earlier, I would rather find water that has a slight riffle so that the leader and tippet wakes that form when you are stripping do not tip the fish off to the imitation. Even though the real caddis on the water rarely stop for a breath, I like to strip three to five times and then rest the fly for a few seconds before resuming the twitching

A Goddard Caddis dry fly. For stillwater fishing, trim the hackle along the bottom so the fly rides low in the water.

retrieves. The takes are usually aggressive and the hook sets can result in broken tippets if you do not control yourself. It's hard not to get excited when the fish rises to your offering but a slow lift of the rod instead of a quick hook set will result in more hookups and fewer broken tippets.

Many of the caddis imitations fished today are heavily dressed with hackle to keep them afloat in the currents and riffles in rivers and streams. If you have bought a traditional Elkhair or Goddard Caddis, trim the hackle along the bottom so the fly sits low on the water. On a stillwater you don't need the hackle to keep the fly from sinking in the current. If you tie your own, I recommend tying caddis imitations for stillwater with hackle palmered only around the front third of the body. I then trim this hackle flat on the bottom of the fly so that the fly sits fully onto the water's surface. Stillwater trout have plenty of time to inspect your offering, and I have found that sparsely dressed patterns perform much better than heavily dressed ones. A fly that is too fully dressed and sitting too high in the water is often refused, where a sparse pattern is quickly consumed.

Patterns that you should start with for stillwater trout fishing include the following:

Nymphs

Beadhead caddis nymphs, No. 12 to 18 in olive, tan, brown, and cream.

Caddis soft hackles, No. 12 to 18 in olive, cream, tan, and black.

Lafontaine Sparkle Pupa, No. 12 to 16 in brown and olive.

Travis Glass Bead Caddis Emerger, No. 12 to 20 in olive, tan, and gray.

Dry Flies

Elkhair Caddis, No. 12 to 16 in tan, olive, and brown.

Black Elkhair Caddis, No. 14 to 20.

Goddard Caddis, No. 10 to 16.

CDC adult caddis, No. 16 to 20 in cream, gray, and olive.

Schroeder's Hi-Vis Caddis, No. 12 to 16.

Henryville Special, No. 12 to 18.

Mayflies

With around six hundred species in the United States, the mayfly is the cornerstone of fly fishing for trout, and there is more information available on mayflies than on all other insect species put together. There are four main types of mayflies: burrowing, clinging, swimming, and crawling. Each has a distinct body shape that correlates with the species. Burrowers and swimmers are the most common mayflies in stillwaters.

Trout feed actively upon the nymphs either opportunistically or while fish are cruising or rooting around

A mayfly dun, *Ephemera guttulata*.

the bottom. During periods of emerging activity, trout won't look at anything else. A good swimming mayfly nymph imitation like a Zug Bug or a Hex Nymph (a burrower yet readily available as a nymph, it has a similar gill and body structure to its swimming cousin) is generally the most successful stillwater pattern to use when prospecting for trout. Their constant activity makes them a stable food source for many stillwater trout. Areas close to shore, shoals that create shallow areas, coves, and points of land are all good starting points when looking for mayfly activity.

Because of the diversity of the mayflies, emerging activity takes place in several different ways. Some crawl out to emerge along the shoreline, while still others emerge subsurface and float to the top before flying off. But the majority swim or float to the surface to emerge in the water's surface film, bringing about the rising activity typically associated with mayflies. This diversity means hatches can take place almost anywhere, depending on which species are active during the season you are fishing. Make sure to note the area, season, and time of day where you find high activity, as this can be cross-referenced for next year or for a neighboring stillwater that you would like to fish.

After emerging, mayflies sitting on top of the water's surface film are called duns, which is the first of two adult winged stages. Their wings are usually dark in color and not quite dry enough to fly away. Duns spend just enough time to dry off their wings, and trout are eager to eat them before they leave the surface. Duns are very susceptible at this time, and their emergence is very exciting for an angler who is ready for it. Be ready early. If the hatch is immense it is hard to fool a fish into taking your offering if it is just one among thousands of real insects on the water.

Duns leave the water and quickly fly to the trees, where they rest for anywhere from a few moments to a few days before starting their mating ritual. At the end of this rest time the adult's thorax will split and the second adult stage, called a spinner, will emerge. Spinners have glossy bodies, clear wings, longer tails, and can be a totally different color than the dun. In this stage the adult is ready to mate and will quickly take flight to find its mate. Fishermen seeing clouds of mayflies gracefully dipping and weaving in the air above the water's surface are witnessing this ritual. As the insects' mating becomes more intense, they will get closer and closer to the surface, where the males will die after mating and the females will finally splay themselves onto the water's surface, releasing their eggs to the bottom before they too die. Trout rising to spinners can barely be seen dimpling the water's surface to inhale the spent mayflies.

Feeding activity starts in deeper water, where fish key on mayfly nymphs that begin their emerging activity by working their way to the surface. In this situation a sinking or sink-tip line works well to fish nymphs close to the bottom. As insects work their way closer to the water's surface you may occasionally see rising trout. Change to a floating line in these situations and work nymphs close to the water's surface. This will often take trout that feed on nymphs just

Mayfly nymph. Stillwater trout feed on the nymphs in deeper water.

prior to the emergence. Dry fly success lies in early detection of this emergence activity. Oftentimes in the middle of a large mayfly hatch, trout become very finicky as to which fly they will take, often refusing your imitation. Casting dry flies early on in these situations will often entice trout to eat your imitation even when rising fish activity is low.

Although mayfly imitations can be intimidating to look at in any dealer's showroom, a few key patterns and sizes will start you on your way with selections that fit many of your fishing situations. Again, like the caddis patterns we described above, patterns that are sparser than stream patterns will produce more fish than those that are heavily dressed.

Here are a few patterns that you should have in your box to start:

Nymphs

Hexagenia nymphs, No. 6 to 10 in olive, natural, and brown.

Zug Bug, No. 8 to 14.

Hare's Ear Nymphs, No. 10 to 18 in olive and natural.

Lepage's Beadhead Hare's Ear, No. 12 to 18.

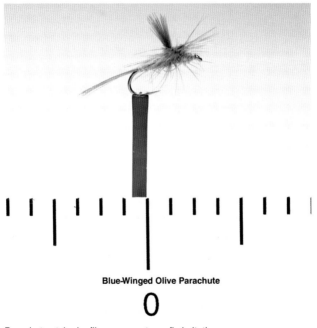

Blue-Winged Olive Parachute

0

Parachute-style dry flies are great mayfly imitations.

Pheasant Tail Nymphs, No. 16 to 22.
Soft-Hackle Hare's Ear, No. 12 to 16 in natural and
olive.

Dry Flies

Parachute Adams, No. 12 to 20.
Quill Gordon, No. 12 to 16.
CDC Mayfly Emerger, No. 14 to 18 in tan, olive,
and brown.
Parachute Red Quill, No. 16 to 18.
Parachute Blue-Winged Olive, No. 14 to 20.
Schroeder's Hi-Vis Hare's Ear, No. 8 to 16.

DIPTERA (MIDGES, GNATS, CRANE FLIES, MOSQUITOES, DEERFLIES)

Easily one of the largest orders of interest to fly fishermen with over eight thousand species in North
America, these insects are an important food source
on stillwaters. The midge family holds the most interest for fly fishermen. Midges can make up as much as
fifty percent of all the invertebrates in any lake or
stream. It's no wonder they are an important food
source for trout, although they are probably among
the food sources most misjudged by fly fishermen.
Often much smaller than anything in your fly box,
midges can be difficult to fish, but their abundance
makes them important. Most midges require less than
a year to emerge. In fact, only a few weeks may
elapse between the egg and adult stages of these

insects. If there is open water you will find midge activity, at any time of year.

Midge larvae are wormlike and can be fished dead drift or with slow strips along weed beds or structure. I have found the most successful way to fish the larvae is by spotting fish along the banks and intercepting them with a cast placed just a few feet in front. Just let the fly sink slowly in front of the fish. Trout will almost always eat your offering as they swim near it. You will often see clouds of midges along the shoreline when activity is highest. Trout seen slurping at what appears to be nothing along the surface are probably feeding on midges. Trying to spot them on the water will take practice, but carefully scanning the surface for these tiny insects will reveal their size, shape, and color. I don't recommend prospecting with midges if you are not seeing trout rising or cruising for nymphs, but fishing midges either wet (when fish can be seen cruising in the shallows), or dry (when fish are consistently rising to the emerging insects) can be productive. During these times trout will often refuse everything offered unless it imitates the midges they are feeding on. Having a few good patterns in your selection makes for some great technical fishing. Present your fly on light tippet; 6X is often too big, and going to 7X and even 8X on these occasions is important for the right presentation. Once hooked up, the challenge of bringing a big trout to net on such small-diameter tippet is the ultimate in stillwater fishing.

When selecting your pattern, size is key as many of these tiny morsels are smaller than a No. 24 hook, although I have seen midges as large as No. 14. The most common ones are between No. 18 and No. 22. Color is the second consideration as midges come in a wide range of colors, most commonly blood red, brown, black, tan, and olive. Midges often cluster up on the water, so having a fly that represents several flies locked together can be productive, and allows you to fish a slightly larger pattern. A Griffith's Gnat is a great dry fly to start with if you are struggling with what to tie on. It is a simple pattern but one of the frequent producers during midge hatches. Carry several sizes so you can readily match the size the trout are feeding on.

Here are a few patterns that I have found successful on those days when you see trout feeding on midges.

Nymphs

Crystal Midge, No. 16 to 20 in olive, tan, and black.
Midge Pupa, No. 16 to 22 in olive, black, and tan.
Brassy, No. 18 to 24.
Buckskin, No. 16 to 22.

Dry Flies

Emergers, No. 16 to 22 in gray, tan, cream, black, and olive.
Griffith's Gnat, No. 16 to 22.
Midge Cluster, No. 16 to 22.
Travis Para Midge, No. 16 to 22.

TERRESTRIALS

During certain times of the year you will find beetles, ants, crickets, and grasshoppers scattered on the water's surface. Usually underestimated by anglers, terrestrials are often overlooked as a food source for trout. These insects find themselves either falling or blown onto the water's surface. Struggling to get back to shore, they are often eaten by rising trout. Although much of this activity takes place close to shorelines as beetles fall off trees or grasshoppers get blown into the water from grassy shorelines. I have seen flying ant hatches that cover the surface, with ants flying far out over the water, where they fall and are snatched by

Terrestrials such as grasshoppers are often overlooked by stillwater trout anglers.

cruising trout. Keeping an eye on the water and sky while you're fishing is a good way to detect this activity early.

Grasshoppers can be cast and slowly stripped back to your position, while ants and beetles are best fished on a dead drift. I have found CDC to be a great underwing material for stillwater ants, beetles, and other terrestrials. It is such a light, fluid material that even fished dead drift it moves, imitating the legs of beetles and ants as they struggle on the water. This often gets the attention of finicky trout as they cruise slowly looking for these helpless victims. These are great prospecting patterns and can be fished even when you do not see any activity on a pond. I have found many stillwaters productive when I strip a grasshopper slowly along the water's surface, even when there is no apparent surface activity.

Flies

Ants, No. 12 to 16 in red and black.
Quick Sight Foam Ant, No. 14 to 18 in black.
Schroeder's Hi-Vis Hopper, No. 8 to 14.
Dave's Hopper, No. 8 to 12 in tan and green.
Grasshoppers, No. 8 to 14 in yellow, green, and brown.
Beetle imitations, No. 12 to 16 in black and green.

STONEFLIES

Stoneflies require highly oxygenated water. This means you will find the highest concentration of these insects along shorelines where wave action beating the banks provides the oxygen necessary for them to survive. Nymphs will live up to four years before drifting or migrating to the shoreline to emerge. Once there, they crawl onto banks, boulders, logs, and so forth to complete their transformation to adulthood. Some larger species like the eastern giant black stonefly will crawl to the top of the highest tree on the bank before emerging as a very large adult. Stonefly nymphs can be differentiated from mayfly nymphs by their pronounced split tails and two well-developed sets of wing pads. They range in size from a couple of millimeters to a couple of inches in length. Although these flies stay well hidden along the bottom, trout will feed on them whenever the opportunity arises, so nymphs fished along shorelines and bottom structure will often take trout looking for a meal.

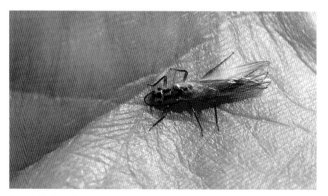

An adult stonefly.

At maturity the nymph's skin splits and the adult emerges. In some smaller species of stoneflies this can happen on the water's surface as with mayflies, but most species crawl out of the water to emerge. During the nymphs' migration to shore they are vulnerable to predatory trout. The winged adults, often emerging in large numbers and being clumsy fliers, will often find themselves blown back into the water, prey for waiting trout. The adults will live a few days, seeking a mate by drumming on leaves. The vibrations are answered by neighboring stoneflies until they eventually get close enough to mate. Females will then either fly over the water, or crawl into the water to release their eggs. This is another time they are susceptible to being eaten.

Large nymphs should be fished close to bottom structure. Use floating line with sinking fly if you are fishing close to shore, and a full-sinking line if fishing off a deep drop-off along a shoreline. The key is to keep the fly close to bottom. I find a slow, deliberate strip along the bottom imitates a crawling nymph and works better than quick, streamer-style, retrieves. Be ready for a heavy hit, as cruising trout often take these flies aggressively.

Nymphs

Kaufmann's Stone, No. 2 to 10 in brown and black.
Beadhead Giant Stone, No. 4 to 10 in brown and black.

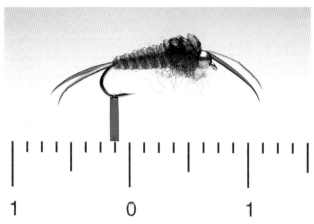

A Beadhead Giant Stone, great for fishing close to bottom structure.

Montana Nymph, No. 8 to 14 in yellow.
Oliver Edwards Little Black Stonefly, No. 12 to 16 in black.
Stonefly Bugger, No. 6 to 10.

Dry Flies

Stimulator, No. 6 to 16 in yellow, orange, and olive.
Schroeder's Hi-Vis Stonefly, No. 10 to 16.
Large Elkhair Caddis, No. 8 to 14 in olive, brown, and black.
Trude, No. 8 to 14 in brown, black, and olive.

Damsels and Dragons

These are among the oldest insects on the planet. It is said that the Odonata order was around to see the coming and going of the dinosaurs. In fact fossils of dragonflies have been found with wingspans in excess of twenty-seven inches. Try to cast that one! The nymphs live from a few months to five years under water before emerging as adults. Nymphs are voracious carnivores and will readily feed on other nymphs, as well as fish fry. Because of their size they are a great food source for trout, and are often eaten as fish root along the bottom trying to dislodge or expose one of these nymphs. So fishing the nymphs close to the bottom is the ticket.

Their three paddle-shaped gills at the end of their long slender abdomens easily identify damsel nymphs, while dragonfly nymphs are short, squat insects that look like goblins. Colors range from drab olive to tan, brown to gray. Damsels are good swimmers and will migrate long distances below the water's surface to arrive at a suitable emerging location. This swimming activity brings trout up to feed aggressively during these migrations. Dragonflies, on the other hand, are too awkward and bulky for swimming so are usually found crawling along the bottom or on vegetation in search of food or an exit site for their emergence.

Both species crawl out of the water to emerge either along the water's edge or on vegetation floating in the water. I have often found dragonfly cases on my tent thirty to forty feet away from the water, where they emerged as adults. Once they have emerged, damsel- and dragonflies can be seen cruising above a stillwater in their brightly colored winged adult form, waiting to snatch whatever insect happens by. I welcome them when mosquitoes or black flies are buzzing around my head, as they play the part of vigilantes when biting insects are in the area. These carnivorous yet beautiful insects live a long life above and below the water's surface. Both are best fished as nymphs, although damselfly adults can bring trout to the surface when depositing eggs. Males attached to females will fly to surface vegetation where the male will release the female, who then crawls to the bottom to release her eggs. She then floats back to the surface, where the male reattaches himself to her and carries her away. They are vulnerable to hungry trout at this stage. Although I have found the nymph to be a more successful pattern to fish, I know fly fishermen who love to fish damsels dry.

Damselflies, being swimmers, can be fished with either a sink-tip or a floating line. I like to make the nymph appear to be moving toward the water's surface as opposed to having it sink during the retrieve. If fishing a floating line, let the nymph sink a bit before starting your retrieve. I often stop midway through my retrieve to let it sink again before finishing my retrieve. With a sink-tip line, let the line sink before starting your retrieve. A sink tip will allow you to fish the nymph through a greater depth of water while still allowing the fly to make its way slowly back to the surface, imitating the emerging or migrating insect.

Dragonflies are bottom huggers and are not found swimming in stillwaters. These nymphs are chunky, and the imitation you choose should match the thickness and width of the dragonflies found in your area. I like to fish these flies on a full-sinking line so that I can retrieve the fly back as close to the bottom as possible. Retrieve these nymphs from deep to shallow water, or toward shore. Wade or anchor close to shore and cast away from you into deeper water, so that the nymph can be retrieved toward shore. Getting hooked on bottom in rocky areas is common when using this technique. One way to lessen your chances of hooking bottom is to fish a full-sinking line with a shorter seven-and-a-half-foot leader and a fly that has neutral buoyancy or a slight amount of flotation. Nymphs tied with deer hair and trimmed to imitate the wide body of a dragonfly nymph tend to stay slightly off bottom when being retrieved. The sinking line will prevent the fly from coming too far toward the surface, while the slight flotation keeps the fly from dragging bottom.

Nymphs

Borger's Damselfly Nymph, No. 8 to 14 in olive, tan, gray, purple, and brown.
Borger's Chenille Dragon, No. 2 to 8.
Assam Dragon, No. 6 to 10 in olive, brown, and gray.

Damsel Dry Fly

Borger's Hair-Wing Damsel, No. 8 to 12 in bright blue, emerald green, olive-tan, and yellow-brown.

STREAMERS, LEECHES, CRAYFISH, AND OTHER BAITS

Stillwaters are home to a variety of food sources for trout, and the baitfish, leeches, and crayfish that are a part of each stillwater are sure to get their attention. These food sources can be a real meal. One redfin shiner, black-nosed dace, or smelt equals many insects in terms of calories ingested. The energy expended to capture them may be higher but the return is great. A box full of different streamers and leech patterns is good to have in your vest when venturing onto any stillwater.

Tiny crayfish are eagerly sought by opportunistic trout.

Streamer patterns imitate baitfish, leeches, and crayfish, and can be fished during any season. I know many good fly fishermen who fish streamer patterns most of the day when on stillwater. The technique used for retrieving a streamer is many times more important than the pattern being fished. I have watched many fishermen who never vary their retrieves when fishing streamers and eventually change patterns, hoping to find one that will trigger a strike.

During a trip with my dad many years ago for land-locked salmon I was fishing a yellow leech, which we had found to be a great fall pattern when these fish were gathering around stream mouths readying themselves for their spawning run. Based on our experiences in this area we felt quite sure fish were gathered in a deep bowl just off the mouth of the stream, but we could not entice a strike after an hour of fishing. After what looked to be a bad cast, when I thought my fly had fouled around my leader, I was retrieving my fly very quickly when I was rewarded with an aggressive strike, and landed a nice salmon. Subsequently deciding that it may have been my retrieve and not just good luck, I changed to very long, very fast strips (as fast as I could move the fly) back to the boat. Instantly our fishing went from nonexistent to a strike on virtually every cast. Another angler fishing in the same area asked what we were using. (Usually this is a final, futile effort by a fly fisherman in any circumstance.) I not only told him the pattern but handed him a couple of our leeches to try out. As he watched us take fish after fish out of the same area, he was frustrated with very little action. It wasn't the pattern, it was the retrieve. This taught me the importance of retrieve over pattern. It can be slow instead of fast, or a variation throughout your retrieve, or a slight flick of your wrist to make the fly twitch at the end of each retrieve, but it is important to experiment each time you fish streamers.

I fish sinking lines 80 percent of the time, but there are times in early spring and in the fall when you can use a floating line. Along shorelines and around stream inlets and outlets, fish are often found cruising when water temperatures allow them to stay in these areas looking for schooled-up bait. You often see fish swirl at your fly as it is being retrieved, which adds to the excitement of fishing streamers close to the water's surface. During the summer months a sinking line fished in deeper water near drop-offs, points, or rocky shoals where water temperatures are cooler will often be your best bet.

Patterns come in a variety of sizes and shapes as either attractors or exact imitations of the bait you are trying to imitate. The attractor patterns (like my Yellow Leech above) are often brightly colored flies that entice fish to strike out of aggression, while the exact imitations are meant to imitate actual baitfish living in the water you are fishing. Attractors like Yellow Leeches, many of the Bugger patterns, and streamers like the Mickey Finn or Red and White do not imitate actual baitfish, yet have been responsible for many

Beadhead Woolly Bugger

1   0   1

The Beadhead Woolly Bugger is a great all-around attractor pattern. You should always have a few in your fly box.

successful outings. I like to prospect with these patterns when fishing activity is slow. Fast stripping of these flies will often entice a strike or at least a follow and swirl. In the spring during smelt runs or other baitfish spawning runs, trout often demand a fly that exactly imitates the bait they are feeding on. Here, try precise imitations like the Grey Ghost streamer, Black-Nosed Dace, or imitations of other baitfish living in the specific water.

Patterns

Woolly Bugger, No. 2 to 8 in yellow, purple, olive, and black.

Black-Nosed Dace, No. 6 to 12.

Grey Ghost, No. 4 to 10.

Black Ghost, No. 4 to 10.

Leeches, No. 2 to 8 in yellow, olive, black, and brown.

Mickey Finn, No. 4 to 8.

INDEX